# The Passion of Nino

## the Enlightener

Credits

Front Cover image –
Icon of Saint Nino at Svetitskhoveli Cathedral, Republic of Georgia
Copyright: Public Domain {PD-old}
Accessed through Wikimedia Commons
*https://eng.ghn.ge/print/10847*

Page iii image of Saint Nino –
by Mikhail Sabinin
Copyright Public Domain {PD-old}
Title: *Saint Nino of Georgia*
Date Created: 1882
Accessed through Wikimedia Commons
*http://catholicsaints.info/wp-content/uploads/img-Saint-Nino-of-Georgia.jpg*

Maps in Appendix –
GNU Free Documentation License, version 1.2 or later
Creative Commons Attribution- ShareAlike 3.0 Unported
Date: 2008
Source: Coppermine Photo Gallery - an open-source project released under the GNU/GPL terms.

Back Cover image –
Copyright: Public Domain {PD-old}
Title: *Saint Nino*
Medium: Painting
Accessed from Wikimedia Commons
*https://upload.wikimedia.org/wikipedia/commons/c/c9/SaintNino.gif*

# The Passion of Nino

## the Enlightener

*A Saint 'Equal-to-the-Apostles'*

*An Inspiring Story Based on Historical Records*

EDWARD N BROWN

CRYSTAL SEA PRESS
CHICAGO, IL

THE PASSION OF NINO
*the Enlightener*



ISBN: 978-1-7367712-4-2
Library of Congress Control Number: 2021913171

Published by Crystal Sea Press, Chicago, IL
*CSP*
*Printed in the United States of America*

For information about this title, or to order other books and/or electronic media, contact the publisher at: rystalse@crystalseapress.com

***This is the story of an ordinary girl –***
***born free, but sold into slavery –***
***powerless and persecuted –***
***oppressed by the harsh twists-and-turns of life –***
***but strong in faith, will, and determination –***
***driven by a Vision of the Virgin Mary –***
***and empowered by Almighty God –***

***She converted Kings and Queens to the one true Faith***
***And she became a Saint – 'Equal-to-the-Apostles'***

***She became the Enlightener of a Nation***

IN THE BEGINNING was the Word,
And the Word was with God,
And the Word was God.
He was in the beginning with God.
All things came to be through Him ...

John 1:1-3

[Bernardo Ramonfaur] © 123RF.com
<'http://www.123rf.com/profile_bernardojbp'>bernardojbp / 123RF Stock Photo>

GLORY BE to the Father,
And to the Son,
And to the Holy Spirit.
As it was in the beginning,
Is now,
And ever shall be.
World without end.
Amen.

The Gloria Patri
A Catholic Hymn of Praise
(also called The Minor Doxology)

# CONTENTS

# CAST OF CHARACTERS

In Order of Appearance (in Nino's Story)

**Zabulon**
Father of Saint Nino and husband of Sosanna

**Gerontius**
Father of Saint George and husband of Polychronia

**Sosanna**
Mother of Saint Nino and wife of Zabulon – sister of Bishop Juvenal

**Polychronia**
Mother of Saint George and wife of Gerontius

**Saint Nino the Enlightener** (as a girl)
[aka Christiana; Nina; Nune; Nano; Nunia]
Daughter of Zabulon and Sosanna

**Saint George the Holy Great Martyr** (as a boy)
Son of Gerontius and Polychronia

**Saint Gregory the Illuminator** (as a boy)
Son of Anak (the Parthian) and Okohe

**Sara Niaphor**
[or Nianfora – Niofora-Sarah – Sara the Hermit]
Caretaker of Saint Nino as a young girl

**Bishop Juvenal of Jerusalem** – [or Houbnal I]
Uncle of Saint Nino

**Blessed Virgin Saint Hripsime** – [or Arsema]
Most beautiful of the Vestal Virgins – daughter of Agatha

**Saint Gayane**
Leader/teacher of the Virgin Community in Rome

**Agatha**
Mother of Saint Hripsime

**Emperor Maximian (the Augustus)**
Emperor of the Western Roman Empire

**Emperor Diocletian (the Augustus)**
Emperor of the Eastern Roman Empire

**Bishop Alexander**
High Bishop of Alexandria

**King Tiridates III of Armenia**
Husband of Queen Ashkhen – Brother of Princess Khosrovidukht

**Saint Gregory the Illuminator** (as a man)
[or Grigor Lusavorich]

**Princess Khosrovidukht**
Sister of King Tiridates III

**Queen Ashkhen of Armenia**
Wife of King Tiridates III

**Awtay**
Foster father of Khosrovidukht

**Levan**
Royal gardener for King Mirian III

**Anastasia**
Wife of Levan

**Davit** (as an infant) – [or Dato]
Son of Levan and Anastasia

**Queen Nana of Iberia**
Wife of King Mirian III

**Abiathar**
Daughter of Jewish servant to Queen Nana

**Perozhavra**
Noblewoman of the Kartli region

**Salome** – [or Beoun]
Wife of Rev II, the son of King Mirian and Queen Nana

**King Mirian III of Iberia**
Husband of Queen Nana

**Rev II**
Son of King Mirian and Queen Nana

**Aspacures II** – [or Varaz-Bakur (or Bakar)]
Son of King Mirian and Queen Nana

**Elioz** – [or Elias]
Trader who brings the Robe of Christ to Iberia

**Sidonia**
Brother of Elioz – buried with the Robe of Christ

**Jacob 'the Priest'**
Accompanied Saint Nino to Kakheti

**Queen Sofia of Kakheti**
Queen of the eastern region of Iberia

# INTRODUCTION

## THE POWER OF THE STORY

**IN** some ways, the age-old act of listening to stories is a lot like examining the nature and operation of physical objects, or looking at and perceiving images (moving or still), or contemplating and reflecting on abstract notions (such as mathematics or literature). The imagination is stimulated, the mental models become mesmerizing, and the excitement is captivating. You are immersed in an alternate reality, like a fantasy or a dream.

Now, there are some extraordinary stories that hold special power over all of us. Ancient and mysterious stories of faith, hope, and courage engage our imaginations – the stories of heroes and their adventures. How they overcame adversity for a just cause forever endures in our collective consciousness. These are stories beset with trouble, calamity, trial, hardship, difficulty, danger, tribulation, and misfortune. But the hero perseveres, and in the end, triumphs over adversity. The characters are plagued with agonizing personal interactions, painful physical afflictions, and harrowing societal oppression. But the real protagonists are the combatants concerned with good and evil, virtue and vice, life and death – with the ultimate choices dictating their behavior – power, fame, and fortune during a short earthly life, or peace, love, and happiness forever in a spiritual life in heaven. These heroes experienced it all and made the right choices. They are role-models, icons, and saints. How they coped with the troubles, conflicts, and dilemmas along the way invigorates our imaginations. These are the stories that affect our souls – stories that we hunger for – because there is a yearning deep within us to want to discover, to understand, and to experience.

For better or for worse, we are influenced by the stories we hear, see, read, and share. That is why the Christian belief, rich in scripture, ritual, and stories of faith, has a deeply formative power. Over time, as we encounter the presence of God in our daily experience, we become what we receive. As darkness settles each night and we prepare to rest for a new day, again and again we turn to stories – in our words, in our thoughts, and in our dreams – to remind us of who we are, what we are, and where we should be going.

Stories have the power to shape us in ways that turn us toward the Good and away from the Bad. Unfortunately, the reverse is also true – and we see the effects every day on TV and in the media. Telling a story is a simple act (although creating a good story is not so simple), but a good story can have positive life-changing consequences – both to the individual and to the world. Sharing a good story, whether by radio, TV, book, computer, or word-of-mouth, helps us understand ourselves, our world, and our proper relationship with God. This then, is the 'Power of the Story'.

## NINO, GEORGE, AND GREGORY

**ABOUT** seventeen hundred years ago, three intrepid heroes came upon the earthly scene at about the same time and in the same place. Aside from a possible informal "hello" in passing-by, they didn't interact much personally. But the actions of George and Gregory did have an effect on the course of events in the life of Nino.[1] All three were born in Cappadocia and raised as Christians.[2] But they went their separate ways as young people caught up in events of the time. Nino went to Palestine and then to Rome, George went to Syria and then to Nicomedia,[3] and Gregory went to Armenia. They each had separate adventures and became exemplars in the early Christian church. Their stories became immensely popular among the common people in the next thousand years, and they were canonized by the formal churches. Saint George developed worldwide notoriety, and is a highly celebrated saint in both the Western and Eastern Christian churches, as well as a prophetic figure in Islamic sources.[4] On the other hand, Saints Gregory and Nino are most readily identifiable with the nations they directly influenced. Saint Gregory the Illuminator is credited with helping to establish Christianity as the official religion of Armenia – consequently, he is recognized as the patron saint of Armenia.[5] Saint Nino the Enlightener is credited with helping to establish Christianity as the official religion of Georgia (called Iberia at the time) – consequently, she is recognized as the patron saint of Georgia.[6]

## SALOME AND PEROZHAVRA

**HOWEVER**, Saint Nino is the centerpiece of this book. Her interactions with Saints George and Gregory are noted in the text, but they are not major players in her life story (although her brief meeting with Gregory, later as a man, was a turning point). But thankfully, everything that did happen in her life was written down for posterity by her close friends Salome and Perozhavra, who were her staunchest allies in her evangelistic efforts. Standing by her deathbed during the last few precious moments of her life, and weeping bitterly at having to part with their beloved teacher, healer, and missionary, Nino related to them her whole life story. The pair had been converted to Christianity by Nino and were determined to see the fruits of her good works continue to thrive, and the spreading of the faith continue to flourish. From the information that Nino related to them, Salome and Perozhavra wrote "The Life of Saint Nino, Enlightener of Georgia".[7] That writing has been lost, but it was read and comprehended by all members of the royal court, and taught to many people in the countryside. Although, in general, stories can become exaggerated and embellished when handed down by oral tradition, the royal court took great pains to make sure that the official story remained pure to the writings of Salome and Perozhavra.[8]

The official story was related verbally by a member of the royal house of Iberia (a prince), named Bakur (Bacurius the Iberian), to a Roman scholar named Tyrannius Rufinus (Rufinus of Aquileia),[9] when they met in Palestine around the year 395 AD. Bakur told him about events that had occurred little more than half a century earlier, during the lifetime of his own parents or grandparents. So, the inevitable time dilution of oral tradition was minimal. Shortly thereafter, Rufinus wrote a chapter on Iberian Church History for the royal government that included the life and ministry of Nino. The writing of Rufinus is still included in the official records of the Georgian royal historical annals. Thus, the legacy of Nino was saved and conserved.

## HRIPSIME AND GAYANE

**THE** parallel story about Hripsime, Gayane, and the 35

Virgins, is extremely popular in the Eastern, Oriental, and Ethiopian Orthodox traditions. They are venerated as the first Christian martyrs of Armenia. Although it's not widely known in the west, some scholars maintain that Christianity became the recognized state religion in the kingdom of Armenia even before it became such in the greater Roman Empire, or in the small kingdom of Iberia.[10] And Hripsime, Gayane, and the others are central to that history, as is the aforementioned Gregory the Illuminator. The role of Nino in the accounts is minor, but critical to the greater history of the region. The whole story is recounted in the book *The History of the Armenians* by Moises Khorenatzi (Moses of Khoren), which was written about the year 440 AD.[11] Hripsime is also highly venerated in Ethiopia, where she is known as Arsema. The book entitled *The Life of Arsema* is found in almost every spiritual bookshop in the country.[12]

## THE CENTRAL STORY

**THE** events in this book roughly take place in the time period 280-340 AD. The story is true according to historical records. However, the various records are not entirely definitive. There are discrepancies and uncertainties in the records that lead to doubts about the total historical accuracy of the details and the dates. Therefore, bounding the time range of events, for the purposes of this book, will suffice in place of scholastic rigor. The events herein certainly happened over the period of time between 280 and 340 AD. But the exact timing of any singular event, or sequence of events, is questionable and subject to endless analysis and debate.

The people and places are real, and the events are accurate – at least as accurate as the available ancient records indicate. But is the story truly non-fiction? Hard to say.

Maybe this is the way it actually played out. Or maybe it's close enough (for government work, as the joke goes) such that the details don't really matter. Like any history and any story, the ultimate truth lies outside the minds of the historian and the storyteller. Those workhands are just conduits of fuzzy historical information from one person to other people. The ultimate historical truth, of course, is known only to God.

The story in this book is a story worth telling. The emphasis is not on the process of how evangelization occurred – nor is it on the day-to-day minutia of dealing with life's problems. The emphasis here is on the faith-based drive of an intelligent, courageous, and resourceful young woman, that had impacts on world history. The story revolves around the rational thought processes that preceded her decisions and actions, and the consequences that resulted therefrom.

Whether myth or history, fact or fiction, one aspect remains – it's a darn good story – a 'tall-tale' like no other! So, what you read in this book is my contribution to the general historical knowledge base. But not just boring dry facts – that's for the academic in a different type of book. For the everyday person – the 'plain Jane' or 'just plain Joe' – I've tried to create an entertaining, yet emotionally fulfilling story line – one that can be thought about, mulled over, or discussed long after the reading is finished. My goal was to fill in the gaps that people often stumble on when reading about historical figures in the mainstream media, not by inventing things from my imagination, but by researching the historical literature and then synthesizing a plausible story thread that, to me, is logically, realistically, and syntactically sound – and one that the reader will enjoy. But, of course, the final judgment is up to you.

## NOTES

---

1. It should be noted that Nino is given the contrived name 'Christiana' in the western Roman Catholic tradition, because the early historical records that attributed to her the name 'Nino' were deemed to be unreliable.

2. Cappadocia is an ancient region in east-central Anatolia (Asia Minor), situated on the rugged plateau north of the Taurus mountains, in the center of present-day Turkey. Rock-cut churches and underground tunnel complexes from the Byzantine era are scattered throughout the countryside. Many abandoned cave dwellings once used as churches and homes for monks in the 14th century (the sprawling underground cities of Derinkuyu and Kaymakli) are now part of Goreme National Park (a UNESCO World Heritage Site). Cappadocia is twice mentioned in the Bible: Cappadocian Jews were present in Jerusalem during the descent of the Holy Spirit on Pentecost (Acts 2:9), and the region is mentioned as a place of dispersed Christian communities in Asia Minor (1 Peter 1:1).

3. Nicomedia was an ancient Greek city located in what is now Turkey. It was rebuilt from ruins by Nicomedes I of Bithynia in 264 BC under the name of Nicomedia, and has ever since been one of the most important cities in northwestern Asia Minor. Nicomedia was a metropolis and the capital of the Roman province of Bithynia under the Roman Empire. It is referenced repeatedly in Pliny the Younger's 'Letters to Emperor Trajan' during the former's tenure as governor of Bithynia. In his letters, Pliny mentions several public buildings of the city, such as a senate-house, an aqueduct, a forum, and the temple of Cybele – and speaks of a great fire, during which the place suffered greatly.

The emperor Diocletian made it the capital city of the Eastern Roman Empire in 286 AD when he introduced the Tetrarchy system of rule. Nicomedia remained as the eastern (and most senior) capital of the Roman Empire until co-emperor Licinius was defeated by Constantine the Great at the Battle of Chrysopolis in 324 AD, and ended the Tetrarchy. Constantine resided mainly in Nicomedia, as his interim capital city, for the next six years, until in 330 AD when he declared the nearby Byzantium, which was renamed Constantinople (modern-day Istanbul), to be the new capital. Constantine died in a royal villa in the vicinity of Nicomedia in 337 AD. Owing to its position at the convergence of the Asiatic roads leading to the new capital, Nicomedia retained its importance even after the founding of Constantinople.

4. Patronages of Saint George exist throughout the world. He is the patron saint of England (his cross features in the national flag of England, the United Kingdom, Australia, and New Zealand), Ethiopia, Georgia (where

365 Orthodox churches are named after him), Malta, Portugal ("Saint George" is the battle cry of the Portuguese Navy), the state of Rio de Janeiro, Catalonia, and Aragon in Spain (The 'Cross of George' emblazons the flags of all Aragon provinces). The widespread attribution to George of the red cross on a white field in Western art – 'Saint George's Cross' – probably first arose in Genoa, which had adopted this image for their flag, and George as their patron saint, in the 12th century. Of course, he is forever immortalized in the legend of 'Saint George and the Dragon'. Reference: https://www.stgeorgessociety.org/news/2018/3/30/saint-george-the-man-the-myth-the-legend.

5. Saint Gregory the Illuminator (c.260 – 330 AD) is not to be confused with Saint Gregory of Nazianzus (c.329 – 388 AD) or Saint Gregory of Nyssa (c.330 – 395 AD). All three were born in Cappadocia and raised as Christians about the same time. However, Gregory of Nazianzus and Gregory of Nyssa, along with Basil the Great (brother of Gregory of Nyssa), are called the 'Cappadocian Fathers' for their championing of Orthodoxy. These three made important contributions to Christian writings, refuting Arianism, and elaborating on the doctrine of the Holy Trinity.

6. Nino goes by other names in other places – she is also known as Christiana, Chrétienne, Nina, Nune, Nuneh, Nano, Ninny, or Nunia.

7. Much of what is present-day Georgia was incorporated in the Kingdom of Iberia at the time (c. 300 AD). Iberia was the land north of Armenia, and was outside the boundary limits of the Roman Empire. Armenia was part of the Empire in 117 AD but later partially relinquished. See the maps in Appendix I. The name of Iberia was later changed to Georgia, presumably derived from the Persian name for the region, 'gurgan', meaning 'land of the wolves'. The popularity of Saint George among the people is unofficially recognized as the source of the change. However, the locals call the country 'Sakartvelo', from the core region of Kartli, which comprised much of ancient Iberia. The constitution of 1995 declared the official name of the nation as Sakartvelo, with the name Georgia as its English equivalent.

8. Salome and Perozhavra are Saints in the Georgian Orthodox Church and the Greek Orthodox Church of Antioch.

9. c. 345–410 AD

10. Sources differ on the exact dates. The date usually given for the Roman Empire is 380 AD (although Christianity was legitimized in 313 AD). The date usually given for Armenia is 301 AD, although considerable controversy exists on this, many thinking that 314 AD is more probable. The dates usually given for Iberia (Georgia) and Ethiopia are 326 AD and 341 AD respectively.

---

11. Reference: Gabriel Soultanian, *The History of the Armenians and Moses Khorenatsi* [London: Bennett & Bloom, 2012].

12. Reference: E.A. Wallis Budge, *The Book of the Saints of the Ethiopian Church*, 4 vols. [Cambridge Univ Press, 1928].

# 1 PRELUDE

**THE YEAR** is sometime around 339 AD.

**THE PLACE** is in eastern Georgia (then called Iberia) in the Kakheti region. Nino has settled in the small village of Bodbe by a mountain pass.

**THE SETTING:** Nino and Jacob 'the Priest' have travelled to the Kakheti region. Joined by her friend Queen Salome,[1] and a bevy of village elders, soldiers, and female slaves, they have converted the people there to Christianity through inspired teaching and baptism. But Nino has fallen sick and is resting in a small village lodge at Bodbe. Her other friend, Queen Perozhavra of the Kartli region has come to help tend to her needs.[2] But her illness has taken a turn for the worse, and there is some concern that she may not recover.

**"I'M** so happy that the people of Kakheti have been brought to see the Light, and have embraced it with such joy and good cheer," whispered Nino to the two queens. "They have accepted Christ's Holy Sacrament and are eager to learn more about the Good News. And I'm so glad that you have finally received the baptism from the priest. We are truly blessed this day." [3]

"Praise be to God," exclaimed Salome. "The people are more hopeful now about the future. Wow, they were really excited when you told them the story of the 'living pillar',[4] and all the marvels surrounding the miracle. Now they know for sure, as I do, that God's hand is present here. It was a glorious day, and I'm burning with desire now to further the Gospel."

After conversion of many of the people from Kakheti, with pride and satisfaction, and a little inspiration from Nino, Salome had gone out and erected a cross in the royal fortified castle at Ujarma, where she and her family live. The cross still stands today. Then she returned to Nino at Bodbe.

"I'm so lucky to have you two by my side as friends and fellow believers. But I must tell you, with all honesty, that I'm not feeling very well at all these days. My stomach hurts and my head aches. And I'm feeling dull all over. I know that I'm in the hands of Almighty God, and what will be with me is what He wills. If I recover, I will give praise to the Lord. But if I don't, I am content that I have done all I can to further His Kingdom, and I will go with the angels cheerfully as a humble servant. In that case, I turn this most important work over to you, my sincerest friends, to keep the momentum and spread the faith."

"Quiet now," said Perozhavra. "Don't talk like that. You are our beloved teacher, healer, and comforter. You came to this country from outside, and have embraced our customs and enlightened our people – you have freed our souls. We don't know anything about your background or how you got here. But we owe you everything. You are part of us now. We will not desert you. Tell us how to continue your good works."

With that, Nino smiles and dozes off. When she awakens a few hours later, she is feeling worse and uncertain about the future. Her breathing is irregular and her voice is cracked and shaky. But she manages to say aloud: "Come to me now, my dearest friends Salome and Perozhavra. Come close and I will tell you everything about my past – my life story – because I believe it has been directed by God. He has given me the gifts, and I have tried to use them according to His wishes. Then you can understand how it all came to be, why I am here, and how I got here. Let me tell you the whole story from the beginning, so you can see how God works on earth in preparation for our life in heaven. Before I pass from this life to the next, I want you to know the story, so that you can pass it on to others, with hopes for their salvation in the glory of Christ, our Lord."

Salome and Perozhavra stood by her bed and wept bitterly, but tried to hide their faces. Then they bent down on their knees and leaned close to Nino. "We will listen to everything you have to say and we will remember. And we will tell all the holy believers about your life in the service of God."

"I have a pen and parchment," added Perozhavra, "and will write down all you say, so nothing will be forgotten or misunderstood."

"My dearest friends, you have my gratitude and my blessing," murmured Nino. "So, I shall tell you my story, as long as I have the breath to tell it. May God grant me the strength to say it all."

"Amen," said the two queens in unison.[5]

And with that, Nino started her story: "It all started in Cappadocia …"

## NOTES

1. Salome of Ujarma was an Armenian princess (from the Arsacid royal family) who was married into Iberian royalty (the Chosroid family). She was a daughter of King Tiridates III and Queen Ashkhen of Armenia. Her birth name was Beoun, but was changed to Salome after she married Rev II of Iberia, the first son of King Mirian III and his second wife, Queen Nana, of Iberia. Through marriage, Salome later became a queen of Iberia, and co-ruled with Rev II and Mirian III.

2. Perozhavra of Sivnia was a noblewoman who was married to the ruler of the Kartli region, an outlying semi-autonomous district that had been evangelized.

3. Prior to converting to Christianity, Salome was a follower of Zoroastrianism, the principal religion of the Persian Empire. She converted and was baptized by Nino, but had just recently received an official baptism by a priest.

4. This story is recounted in Chapter 6.

5. Salome and Perozhavra are Saints in the Georgian Orthodox Church and the Greek Orthodox Church of Antioch. As a dedication to honor the memory of Nino – and as a continuation of her work to spread Christianity throughout Iberia – Salome and Perozhavra wrote a biography on her life, titled "The Life of Saint Nino, Enlightener of Georgia".

# 2 CAPPADOCIA AND PALESTINE

*Go to the country that was assigned to me, and preach the Gospel of our Lord. He will send down His grace upon you, and I will be your protector. I will be for you a shield against all visible and invisible enemies.*

**THE YEAR** is sometime around 339 AD.

**THE PLACE** is in eastern Georgia (then called Iberia) in the Kakheti region. Nino has settled in the small village of Bodbe by a mountain pass.

**THE SETTING:** On her deathbed, Nino is relating her life story to her friends Salome and Perozhavra.

**THE STORY LINE:** The story begins in central Turkey (then called Cappadocia) with the birth and early life of Nino's father and mother.

### CHILDHOOD

"**MY** father was named Zabulon and he was born and raised in Cappadocia.[1] His best friend was a lad called Gerontius, and they were always hanging out together. When they were in their late teen years, seeking adventure like many their age, they decided to join the army and see the world. Being intelligent and quick-witted, they quickly became officers and were posted to Palestine within a year. It was in Palestine that both my father and his buddy met the women they would shortly marry. I think that they were there for about two years. As their tour of duty in Palestine was coming to an end, they both tied the knot in a dual ceremony with little fanfare. My father married Sosanna, who would become my mother, and Gerontius married a woman named Polychronia. As my father later expressed to me, they were all very happy in Palestine. It was peaceful, the economy was good, and they rambled around the region enjoying themselves. But only a few months after the wedding ceremony, the army shipped them back to Cappadocia – and the wives accompanied them."

"I was born in the mostly-Greek town of Kolastra,[2] Cappadocia, about a year later. My parents were very proud and our life, for the most part, was quiet and happy. About the same time – I'm not sure exactly when – Gerontius and Polychronia had a boy, and they named him George.[3] Sometimes we played together, but he was very moody and more of a loner. I don't think he had many friends. But even then, I recognized that George was special somehow – I always thought that he would become a great man – I wonder how he turned out.[4]

"There was also another slightly older boy who would come around once in a while from a neighboring village, named Gregory.[5] He had some relatives in our town. He treated us as silly little kids, but we kind of thought of him as a 'big man about town'. I saw him again years later in Armenia, and he was doing wonderful things for God and the Church.

"Sometime during this period, my father converted to Christianity. I'm sure that Sosanna was the evangelist, since her father was the bishop of Jerusalem.[6] Children of religious parents rarely marry pagans willingly, unless they detect an innate goodness in the person, and the real possibility of bringing him or her into the fold. I know that my mother saw this in my father. So, I was raised in a loving Christian family, and my childhood was uneventful."

## MOVE TO PALESTINE

"**WHEN** I was nine years old, my father decided that the family should move back to Palestine. It was because of a combination of things, I think. Religious persecution against Christians in the Empire was increasing, and my family was worried about the local governor. Also, my father's parents had passed away, and it was a chance for my mother to be with her relatives again. Plus, my father was becoming more and more interested in the faith, and he wanted to see the holy sites in Palestine. Since his mandatory service time with the army was up, he resigned his commission. We sold most of our possessions, packed up what little we had left, and shipped off to Jerusalem in Palestine."

"Life was tougher there. I didn't have many friends, and we didn't have much money to go places or do things. One day, my father announced that after much thought and deliberation, he decided that he wanted to fully enter Christ's service as a monk. My mother and I didn't know what to say, so we just went along with it matter-of-factly, to see how it would play out. But after a few months, we could tell that he was serious. He said that he was going to enter a hermitage and lead an ascetic life as a servant of Christ. I didn't know what that meant, but I didn't want him to leave. We were a simple but happy family, and I didn't want that to change. Nevertheless, a few months later he left us with just the shirt on his back – off he went to a monastery. We thought he might come back in a few weeks or months. But he never did – I never saw my father again. They said he went to labor in the wilderness of the Jordan, but I don't really know.

"After my father left, my mother was greatly troubled. She couldn't take care of me and work a job at the same time. Her father saw her pain, and under his authority as bishop, ordained her into the ministry and made her a deaconess. In this role, she had to spend much time in the church and in travelling to comfort the believers. Since she had no time to properly care for me, an elderly woman from the church was found to be my caretaker. Her name was Nianfora,[7] but I called her Sara – I liked her very much. She was of Armenian descent, had moved to Bethlehem when young, and had been prominent in the church in Jerusalem for a long time. She was known to be very wise – especially in the faith and in the words of Scripture. We bonded closely, and she taught me everything about God the Father, God the Son, and God the Holy Spirit. For the next two years I studied hard, prayed, and worked for the glory of God. I missed my mother and father, but I was otherwise happy and content living with Sara, listening to her wisdom, and learning all that I could about the faith."

## THE CALLING

"**IT** was Sara who told me about the Robe of Christ; how by the rolling of dice, it was allotted to a Roman soldier,[8] then sold to a Christian convert, and then finally brought to Iberia as a present – a land mostly of pagans [9]– but it was subsequently buried and lost. I was fascinated by the story, and dreamed of being able to go there someday and search for the Robe myself – and to find it by the grace of God! I never forgot that story, or lost that desire. I began to pray fervently to God, and to the Virgin Mary, asking for blessings to travel to Iberia, find the Robe, and be made worthy to venerate the sacred relic.

"Then, one night I had a dream – and the Virgin Mary

appeared to me clear as day. Then she said to me:

> *Go to the country that was assigned to me by lot [10]– it is called Iberia – and preach the Gospel of our Lord Jesus Christ. He will send down His grace upon you, and I will be your protector. I will be for you a shield against all visible and invisible enemies.*

"Overwhelmed at the thought of such a great responsibility, I answered meekly, 'How can I, a fragile girl, perform such a momentous task? For that matter, how can I believe that this vision is real?'

"In response, as a pledge of protection, she presented me with a sacred cross made from grapevines, and proclaimed:

> *By the strength of this cross, you will erect in that land the saving banner of faith in my beloved Son and our Lord.*

"When I awoke in the morning, I was holding that very cross in my hands. I was choked with emotion. Shaking with excitement, I dampened the cross with tears of rejoicing, and bound it together securely with strands of my own hair. I tied the cross in my hair that very day, and went to visit my uncle, bishop Juvenal, to tell him about the dream and show him the cross. Although I was only a simple young girl, I revealed to him my desire to preach the Gospel in Iberia. I think I was 11 years old.

"Bishop Juvenal was surprised, curious, cautious, apprehensive, excited, and thankful to God, all at the same instant. He didn't waste much time. After praying a lot that night, he came to me the next day, saying, 'Come my child – you have received the grace of God – it is time to give you the blessing. I don't pretend to understand the ways of God – how such a young girl can preach the Gospel, or travel the world, or withstand the slings and arrows of cruelty and abuse – but if you have been chosen by God, then who am I to interfere? The cause is just and the rewards are great. We put our faith in God and He will not fail us. You will probably encounter trials and tribulations, but I know He will be with you always, wherever you go. So, I give you my blessing, and with all of my heart, the commission to go forth and spread the Gospel.'

"Then, he led me into the church and up to the holy altar. Placing his hands on my head, he prayed the following words:

*O Lord, God of Eternity, I beseech You on behalf of my orphaned niece: Grant that she may go and preach the Gospel, according to Your will, proclaiming the Holy Resurrection. O Christ God, be to her a companion, teacher, guide, refuge, and spiritual father. And, as You did enlighten the Apostles, and all those who praised Your name, also enlighten her with the wisdom to proclaim Your glad tidings. Give her the holy words with force and wisdom, such that no one will be able to oppose or refute them.*

*And I pray to our most Holy Virgin Mother of God, Helper and Intercessor for all Christians – clothe this girl, who you have chosen to preach the Gospel of our Lord Jesus Christ among the pagan nations, with the girdle of strength to overcome all enemies, visible and invisible. Be always for her a shield and an invincible protector – do not deprive her of your favor until she has fulfilled your holy will.*

*Lord God, Our Savior! As I let this young girl depart to preach Your Divine Goodness, I commit her into Your hands.*

"A few weeks later, he told me that he had made arrangements to travel to Rome – and that I should accompany him. It was primarily for church business, but he said that it would be a good place to make the needed contacts, and all the necessary preparations, for the journey to Iberia. I was unbelievably excited. Of course, I insisted that both my mother and Sara travel with us. But he told me that my mother had fallen ill while on church travel to Antioch, and that she needed time to recover. I think he knew that my mother was much weaker than he let on – he didn't want me to fret about being with her to comfort her – and I believe that my mother told him exactly what he should say. She loved me, and she loved God – she wanted me to go and fulfill my destiny without reservation – that was just the way she was. I had not seen her for three weeks. And, although I did not know it then, I would never see her again.

"But bishop Juvenal reluctantly agreed to let Sara accompany us. Sara felt that she was too old to travel and didn't relish the trip, but on the other hand, she felt a strong responsibility to protect, nurture, and guide me during my formative years – especially at this critical time. I suspect she knew about my mother's health, but never said anything. Instead, she focused on teaching and guiding me in the ways of life and in the ways of God."

"A few weeks later, the three of us – my uncle Juvenal, Sara, and myself – travelled to the port of Caesarea, and then set sail for Rome."

## NOTES

---

1. Cappadocia is an ancient district in east-central Anatolia (Asia Minor), situated on the rugged plateau north of the Taurus mountains, in the center of present-day Turkey. Rock-cut churches and underground tunnel complexes from the Byzantine era, and earlier, are scattered throughout the countryside. Many abandoned cave dwellings once used as churches and homes for monks in the 14th century (the sprawling underground cities of Derinkuyu and Kaymakli) are now part of Goreme National Park (a UNESCO World Heritage Site). Cappadocia is twice mentioned in the Bible: Cappadocian Jews were present in Jerusalem during the descent of the Holy Spirit on Pentecost (Acts 2:9), and the region is mentioned as among the dispersed Christian communities of Asia Minor (1 Peter 1:1). Three prominent theologians in the 4th century hail from Cappadocia: Basil the Great, Gregory of Nyssa, and Gregory of Nazianzus – they all made important contributions to Christian writings, refuting Arianism, and elaborating on the doctrine of the Holy Trinity.

2. 'Kolastra', 'Colostra', and 'Colastri' are found in the records. It is not the same as Colossae (from which comes the New Testament Book of Colossians), which is in Phrygia about 100 miles east of Ephesus. There are some unverified claims that the present-day town is called 'Ortahisar' (Turkish for 'middle castle'), aptly named because of the relatively big castle there in the middle of town. It lies in the Nevsehir region in Turkey. There is a small unassuming church here carved out of the rock on her supposed birthplace. A dilapidated sign hangs on the wall inscribed "Nino was born here" (in Turkish). It's not far from Ortahisar Castle, a large rock formation of living and working spaces (some hewn into the rock and some attached or adjacent to the rock face). However, the claims that Nino was born in Ortahısar may be nothing more than commercialism. Although the ruin is definitely a Christian church (given the architecture and the unrestored decaying painted images of Jesus and the parents of Mary), there is no substantiated linkage to Nino's birthplace. Of course, as hoped, the designation has promoted some tourism, as Georgian officials and tourists from everywhere visit the site. Often, they leave behind hand-written prayers and cardboard icons.

3. The Holy Great Martyr George - best known by the moniker 'Saint George and the Dragon', for his part in the slaying of a fierce beast that was terrorizing the city of Silene (now in Libya). The lance with which George slew the beast was called 'Ascalon', after the ancient city of Ashkelon, today in Israel. Interestingly, the name 'Ascalon' was used by Winston Churchill for his personal aircraft during World War II.

4. Of course, the rest is history, as they say. Reference: https://www.independent.co.uk/life-style/st-georges-day-google-doodle-england-patron-saint-soldier-dragon-a9479816.html, for more on the life story of Saint George.

5. Saint Gregory – best known by the term 'Gregory the Illuminator', for his central role in bringing Christianity to Armenia. Reference: https://www.independent.co.uk/life-style/st-georges-day-google-doodle-england-patron-saint-soldier-dragon-a9479816.html, for more on the life story of Saint Gregory.

6. Various sources list Sosanna's father's name as Juvenal or Houbnal I.

7. also called Sara Niaphor, Niofora-Sarah, or Sara the Hermit

8. Reference Matthew 27:35, Mark 15:24, Luke 23:34, and John 19:23-24.

9. The holy Apostles Andrew (the First-Called), Simon the Zealot (Simon the Canaanite), and Matthias were the first to bring the Gospel to Iberia. This was done shortly after leaving Jerusalem, in response to Jesus's command to go out and spread the Gospel to the ends of the earth. But their spiritual inroads were meager. A few embraced the new faith, but most of the pagans were contemptuous of the new religion.

10. After Pentecost, the 12 apostles, and many of the disciples, drew lots to determine who would go where (two-by-two per Jesus' directive [Mark 6:7]) to spread the Gospel to the ends of the earth. Mary, the mother of Jesus, and the other staunch women disciples, partook in the drawing of the lots. Mary was to go to Iberia. But she had been held back from going because of concern for her safety. However, in a dream, she was assured that someone would later enlighten it in her place.

# 3 ROME

*In the community of Vestal Virgins there was one named Hripsime – and she was like no other – unrivaled in beauty, grace, stature, and composure.*

**THE SETTING:** On her deathbed, Nino is relating her life story to her friends Salome and Perozhavra.

**THE STORY LINE:** Nino, Sara, and her uncle, Bishop Juvenal, have arrived in Rome and are settling in. Life-changing events are about to take place.

### ORPHANED

"**THE** sea voyage was tough on Sara. She needed a lot of rest when we finally arrived at our room in the visitor's annex of the nondescript church building, where we were staying and my uncle was working. I continued to read and study my lessons and say my prayers during this time, although I admit, that I occasionally sneaked out to glimpse the mysteries of the city. My uncle brought me to some men who were supposed to organize the details of a future trip to Iberia. But the particulars and logistics made my head spin. I was overwhelmed by all the facts and figures – it seemed like a major undertaking. But I wanted to go, and if this is what was required to get there, then so be it. I smiled and said 'OK' most of the time.

"After two or three weeks of this tedium, my uncle came to me solemnly one morning and told me that he had just gotten a message that my mother had died. She had died in the grace and service of Almighty God, and all the proper Christian rites had been administered. I cried for two days, but Sara consoled me, and we slowly went about our normal daily activities, albeit in mourning and sorrow. My uncle explained to me that she was now with God in heaven, and would be with us again someday. This took the edge off, but I was still sad.

"He also said that all the preparations for the trip would be ready in another month or so, and then I would be able to depart on my journey. He had personally selected my escorts and was confident in their ability and integrity. I was both excited and depressed at the same time. Sara gave me the names and addresses of her relatives in Armenia, which was on one of our stopovers, and I assured her that I would make contact and give them her regards.

"Sara was very happy that I might get to see her relatives, but her health was continuing to decline. I think she felt that her mission to raise me up as a just servant of God was nearing completion. Two weeks later she succumbed to the ills of travel, age, and health, and died peacefully in her sleep – and now I was mourning both my mother and my caretaker. I felt terribly lonely, and lost all excitement and motivation to go on the journey. Deep down, I still wanted to go, but it just felt wrong leaving amid the grief and sadness."

"As it turned out, I didn't have to make any decisions. Events of the day overtook all of our plans. Apparently, there was a new persecution of Christians in Rome, and everyone was in a tizzy. All the church workers had to disperse quickly out of the city and into the countryside – the more remote, the better – or face arrest, or worse. My uncle was forced to go undercover and catch a ship back to Palestine in two days – in steerage – and there was only room for one.

"I had to be left in Rome. Since there was no one to care for me, and no place for me to stay, my uncle had me placed in an orphanage for girls. And although it was a good facility, I felt alone and abandoned. He admirably explained everything to me, but I was miserable. All my hopes and dreams had now gone down the drain. Everything had fallen apart. The next day, my uncle boarded the ship for home, and I was left in a strange, crowded, and unruly place on my own. Rome had turned into a nightmare. But the nightmare was not yet over."

## THE CLERGY OF VESTAL VIRGINS

"**THE** girls in the orphanage were mostly runaways and truants. They were not delinquents or criminals, but they were not at all well-behaved or well-mannered either. They were mostly all pagans, and I was shocked and appalled at their lack of piety and reverence for created things, living or not. Their souls were tormented, and I became very distressed at their lack of devotion to the one true God, and our Lord Jesus Christ. I tried to administer to them on a number of occasions, but they always just rebuffed me, saying something like, 'What's wrong with you? Are you an atheist or something?'[1] It was depressing, but I tried to keep up my daily prayers and meditations in the few private moments I could find."

"Then, one day, a few months later, we had some visitors. It was a group of five women from the Clergy of Vestal Virgins. As you probably already know, these were women who had dedicated themselves to the goddess Vesta.[2] One of their main jobs was to tend to the eternal flame in the temple, but they had other community roles,[3] and one was to visit the orphanages and give comfort to the resident girls and young women. Two of the group were vestals-in-training, two were vestals-in-waiting,[4] and one was the chaperon. They told us about their duties and how important they were to a healthy society [5]– and then asked around to see if anyone was interested in joining. Most of the girls of age listened halfheartedly or paid little attention. A life of virginity for 30 years held little appeal, even if they did receive certain freedoms and legal rights.[6]

"However, they noticed that I listened intently. Of course, I hated their admiration and veneration of a pagan god, but I took notice of the liberties and lifestyle perks that they enjoyed. And so, they talked to me and I talked to them. I was about 12 years old at the time. Every few weeks they would return, and we would talk. They soon realized that I was a Christian, but they didn't threaten to inform on me. The two women that seemed to be the most interested were named Hripsime and Gayane, and we had very good conversations. Both were older than 12 and Gayane was the oldest, not counting Agatha, who was Hripsime's mother and the chaperon. Gayane seemed to be in charge of the vestals-in-waiting.

"Over the next few months, I told them more and more about the one true God, about Jesus Christ our Lord, and about the Holy Spirit come on earth. I told them all about the virgin birth, the miracles, the crucifixion, and the resurrection – and I told them that they too could be saved and resurrected with eternal life. Finally, one day they asked what it would take for them to receive the blessing of conversion. This must have been a carefully considered inquiry because all the other priests and priestesses in the Clergy were devout pagans, and such an act would be considered unthinkable. It would surely mean expulsion from the Clergy, and very likely many societal difficulties, if not outright punishment of some kind. I told them that baptism by a Christian priest, accompanied by a deaconess,[7] was the way to go, but we never got a chance to follow-up on it."

## THE OBSESSION WITH HRIPSIME

"**AT** that time, Maximian was the emperor of the western empire,[8] although many thought that Diocletian, the emperor of the east, exerted the real power. Maximian was obsessed with finding the most beautiful maiden in all of the empire, such that she could be his wife in marriage. So, he enlisted a contingent of the best painters to depart into every region, seek out and find the most beautiful maidens, and paint a picture of them, complete with all of their bodily attributes, proportions, and charms – so as to allow him to review them all and choose the one whom he found the most appealing.[9] When those painters arrived in Rome, they found the temple of Vesta, and the associated community of ascetics. When they came to check out the maidens there, per the imperial directive, they discovered the vestal named Hripsime – and she was like no other – unrivaled in beauty, grace, stature, and composure.

"Now, it so happens that the painter who composed the picture of the maiden that would eventually be selected by the emperor, would receive a hefty bonus – consequently, they were all eager to paint the picture of Hripsime. And that is exactly what occurred. I don't think Hripsime understood all the ramifications of the contest – and I'm sure she wasn't happy about it – but she dutifully posed for the paintings, since it was by order of the emperor.[10] After a few days, the paintings were collected – six or seven, I think – and sent to the emperor, along with all their other paintings of other maidens collected en-route."

"When the emperor saw the paintings of Hripsime a few weeks later, he became very excited – he had found the one for him – the next empress. And so, he notified the temple priest of his decision, and sent an invitation to all the regional governors to come to Rome for the wedding ceremony, which was to be in three weeks' time. Of course, there was no thought that anything could sidetrack the wedding plans. When the clergy and community of the temple learned about this, many were happy for the girl – after all, this was a big deal, a grand future. But most of the vestals were sad. They didn't want to lose their friend, and didn't want her to forsake her vows. But they didn't know what to do.

"When asked whether this was what she really wanted in life, after some reflection Hripsime calmly said 'no'. She was a quiet, humble person, and did not crave the limelight or the fame. But she also did not know if there was anything that she could do. Outright refusing the emperor would be an act of treason, and she could be sorely punished, or even executed. It was from the leader Gayane, that a solution emerged. She asserted that the only reasonable course of action would be to quietly slip out of Rome, with no forwarding address, and go to a place where they could not be found. It was a risky undertaking – where would they go, how would they get there, who would they contact, etc., etc., etc.? But she was convinced that this was the only way forward. The others agreed, and they started to make plans for the escape. 35 souls in all decided to go together on the trip as one group. I think it amounted to 12 vestals, 10 women, and 13 men, but I can't be sure about the numbers. But they were united in their belief that this was an unjust violation of their sanctity."

"Gayane, Hripsime, and Agatha came to me in the orphanage a few days later and explained the whole sequence of events. It was just a courtesy call, I think. But they were surprised when I blurted out that I really wished that I could join them – leave the orphanage and accompany them to a safe haven. I told them that I had contacts in Armenia, given to me by my foster mother, where they could stay. Of course, I didn't really know if they could stay there – I knew nothing about Sara's relatives – but it just came out of my mouth without thinking. I became nervously excited. Armenia was on the eastern fringe of the Empire, sufficiently remote that they might never be found out, so I said. And they considered it and believed me. It certainly sounded better than any of their other options. And so, they then asked me to join them in the clandestine adventure, not as a full member of their clergy, of course, but as an associate – a co-traveler – and I eagerly accepted. This was all very fortuitous, because my real goal was to reach Iberia, and Armenia was just a short stepping-stone away. I was back on my life's journey.

"That very day, as we were discussing the planning details, I mentioned to them that it was right and just that they be consecrated to Christ instead of to Vesta. Much of their lives would be unaltered. They would still serve the community and perform certain rites, but now the focus would be on the one true God, and the church that praises Him, instead of on the false pagan goddess, and the temple that idolizes her. They saw the logic in my argument, and I was glad for them, but both Gayane and Hripsime really wanted to be baptized – and they wanted to be baptized before they left on the journey, so they could feel assured that Christ was with them. I understood, and said that I would find a suitable priest and deaconess. With that, they left and said they would return in a few days, when the arrangements had been made and it was almost time to depart."

## BAPTISM AND DEPARTURE

"**THREE** days later they returned, saying that departure was set for late the next day. I was packed and ready, but had not been able to find a priest available to perform the baptism – they were all in hiding or had left town because of the persecution. Gayane and Hripsime were very distraught.

"But then I remembered that my uncle had left me two small vials of holy oil and holy water. Although not enough to do a full body anointing and baptism, I reasoned that if I mixed the few available drops of holy oil and water with larger amounts of more readily available liquids, then the resulting mixture should still be holy. Still, there was no holy person to administer the sacrament.

"Then I remembered that in an emergency life-and-death situation, the baptismal rite could be performed by any already-baptized Christian person, with the supposition that if the aspirant survived the deadly ordeal, a proper official baptism would be performed at a later time when conditions were safer. I remembered that there were precedents for this. Indeed, the saintly woman Thecla even baptized herself when she thought that her death was imminent.[11]

"And so, when I explained this to Hripsime and Gayane, and suggested that I could perform a preliminary baptism rite, they were overcome with joy and relief. I'd watched my mother perform the rite a couple of times, so I pretty much knew what had to be done and what had to be said. So, without further ado, I gathered my stuff together and we all went into the bathing room – after making sure that it was private – and I gave the sacrament of baptism to Hripsime and Gayane, using the little bit of holy oil and water available. I must have looked kind of silly – a 12-year-old giving a sacred baptism to a 16-year-old and a 20-year-old – but I stumbled through it without a hitch, and everyone was extremely happy and self-fulfilled. I must say, it was an awesome experience – the Light of the Holy Spirit was never brighter.

"As Gayane and Hripsime were leaving to return to the temple community, they were in great spirits, and mentioned that many other members also wanted to undergo the baptismal rite as soon as possible. They had been quietly talking about this to the community, and all the vestals that were in solidarity with the plan to undertake the journey had expressed the desire to be baptized. That night, all the community members intent on leaving Rome prayed to God to help them on the journey, and to keep them in their chastity. And in my last night in the orphanage, I prayed fervently to God for wisdom, courage, and strength, so that I could help the group escape the oppression of the pagan state, and experience the goodness, mercy, and love of Jesus Christ, our Lord and Savior."

"The next evening, a group of 35 people, each with two bags, met me on a dimly lit side-street. About half the total temple community had decided to follow Gayane and leave Rome. There was no time for rituals or even introductions. I joined them and we headed for the carriages that would take us to the port. Arrangements had been made – at no small risk I might add – and we were booked on a cargo ship to Alexandria that very night. We would have to change ships in Alexandria to get to Antioch in Syria. Then we would have to undergo a long trek northeast through Mesopotamia and Pontica to reach Armenia.

"As we stepped onto the ship, and paid off the porters, I said goodbye to Rome and Italy. I was not afraid – I had a group of 35, and at least two Christians, by my side. I did not know how it would all turn out, but I was excited and eager to start a new stage of my life. And I was now getting closer to Iberia. Right then, I just knew that I would get there and fulfill my dream."

## NOTES

---

1. Uneducated pagans often thought that if you didn't believe in the traditional gods of the Greeks and Romans, then you must not believe in gods at all – you were an atheist. Trying to explain to them the truth of the one true God, and the falsity of their multiple gods, was not an easy task. A skilled orator, like the Apostle Paul, was extremely rare and valuable.

2. Vesta was the virgin goddess of the hearth, home, and family. The goddess was usually visualized by the image of fire, as represented by the fire of her temple. Entry to the temple was permitted only to priestesses, called the vestal virgins. Vesta was considered to be a founding guardian of the Roman people.

3. At varying times there were 4 to 6 full-time priestesses employed by the Clergy, but there were additional part-time vocations, and a contingent of in-training members. Officially, they tended the sacred fire in the shrine of Vesta in the Roman Forum, and performed other rites associated with the goddess, such as caring for the sacred objects in the shrine, preparing ritual food (such as the bread for special feasts and the herbs sprinkled on sacrifices), and officiating at public events during the yearly Vestalia Festival (Vesta's feast days – June 7-15).

4. like a backup or vice-vestal – ready to step in if a primary vestal was sick or injured

5. Altogether, the members of the temple community numbered about 72 (35 virgin women called vestals + 24 older mothers, widows, and spinsters + 13 men, who supported the needs of the full-time Clergy of Vestal Virgins).

6. The vestal virgins were chosen between the ages of 6 and 12 by the chief temple priest and had to serve for 30 years (during which time they, of course, had to remain chaste). Once their 30 years of service was completed, they were free to marry or live however they wished (but very few did so). Most continued in strict observance of a chaste single life, through old age and up until death.

If a vestal virgin failed in her duties, she was punished by the high-priest, who would beat and whip the offender with her clothes removed in a dark place (ostensibly with a curtain drawn between them). The punishment for loss of virginity was to be buried alive (near the gate called Collina, where a little mound of earth now stands), though other worse punishments were sometimes given (pouring molten lead down their throat is mentioned in the records).

---

7. In early Christian baptismal ceremonies, newcomers to the faith were anointed and baptized naked, with a deacon accompanying them down into a pool of water. In the case of female aspirants, simple propriety suggested that a woman should perform this task, since the anointing did not involve merely pouring oil over the candidate's head and shoulders, but was comparable to the way oil was used in Greco-Roman bathing and in athletic contests of the period – the oil was rubbed into the person's skin and over their whole body as a kind of quasi-mystical enhancement. When the baptized woman came up out of the water, the deaconess would cover her and then instruct her in purity and holiness on how the seal of the baptism was unbreakable.

8. The proper term was the 'Augustus'. In the Tetrarchy system of government, which was then in effect, Diocletian was the 'Augustus' (emperor) of the East and Galerius was the 'Caesar' (junior emperor) of the East. Maximian was the 'Augustus' (emperor) of the West and Constantius I (Maximian's adopted son) was the 'Caesar' (junior emperor) of the West.

9. Some sources assign this absurd endeavor to Diocletian, since he was considered by many to be the ultimate authority.

10. It's highly likely that most of the paintings depicted the model in the nude. However, the posing of the model for the painters was most likely not in the nude – they were most probably fully clothed in their finest attire. Forcing women to pose naked would have caused a lot of problems and complications – especially in high-end establishments where the painters were wont to go.

11. Reference: Edward N Brown, "The Passion of Thecla: Faith and Fortitude" [Chicago: Crystal Sea Press, 2020]. Thecla jumped into a pool of poisonous seals to save herself from ravenous lions in the arena. Fearing death on both accounts, she quickly baptized herself in the pool, content in the knowledge that Paul, the Apostle, had promised her baptism in the future. Aided by a sudden violent storm, she survived both tortures, and emerged a hero. Her adventures quickly became the stuff of legend.

# 4 ARMENIA

*I will not forsake my true Bridegroom, the Lord Jesus Christ. I will not renounce my faith. My God is with me now! And I will not defile myself with an unclean pagan! May God have mercy on your soul!*

**THE SETTING:** On her deathbed, Nino is relating her life story to her friends Salome and Perozhavra.

**THE STORY LINE:** Nino and the community of 35 have arrived in Vagharshapat, Armenia, thinking that they have found a safe haven. But such is not to be.

### TRAVEL TO ARMENIA

"**WE** arrived in Alexandria after a grueling sea voyage, and thankfully, had three weeks to recover before sailing for Antioch. We stayed with local Christian families in their homes, and tried to keep a low profile. During that time, we visited the high bishop named Alexander,[1] and all the temple community were baptized – the men, the women, and the vestals. I told the bishop about what happened in Rome, and how I had baptized Gayane and Hripsime. He was understanding and accepted the baptism, but gave them both an additional special blessing. It was a joyous occasion, bringing them all into the community of God."

"After the three weeks, we sailed for Antioch, and arrived there without incident.[2] We were all in good spirits, so the sea voyage seemed pleasant – and the waters were calm, which helped. In Antioch, I very much wanted to go to Jerusalem to visit my uncle, but there just wasn't enough time. We were scheduled to leave on a caravan headed north in five days.[3] There was barely enough time to visit the local bishop and describe our mission. I sent a letter to my uncle in Jerusalem, but I never learned whether he ever received it – I never heard from him again.

"Amazingly, a few pious souls decided to join our intrepid group – they were headed to the far-flung eastern regions of Galatia – or Pontus,[4] as it was sometimes called – to spread the Gospel, and we were going the same direction. Altogether, I think, about 40 believers left Antioch that day."

"We followed rivers and valleys through the mountainous terrain and stopped at villages whenever possible for rest and refreshment. If the local people were friendly and receptive, we preached to them, and many were made aware of the Good News. At most stops, we were able to perform baptisms, and many souls were converted along the way. I was happy to see the Holy Spirit at work – I wished we could have stayed longer and set up churches, but we had to keep moving. Occasionally, two or three hardy souls would ask to join our caravan, and we always obliged. After a month of trekking, I think we had about 50 people in the group.

"After what seemed like an eternity, we reached the border with the Kingdom of Armenia. Some in the party – mostly those who joined in Antioch – had left to go to their desired destinations – I think we were back to about 40 souls. Collectively, we breathed a sigh of relief, as we thought we would now be safe from the clutches of the emperor and his cohorts. Of course, that was not to be the case, as we would later find out."

## INTO ARMENIA

"**EVENTUALLY**, we reached the royal city of Edessa, which was near the border with Armenia.[5] Christian persecution there was strong and we could not stop to socialize with the local Christians or evangelize to the pagans. So, we passed on through to the northern outskirts, where there was a large field and an encampment of rustic nomads.[6]

"They were very friendly and welcomed us, and although their singing and dancing was amazing, they were very poor and had no money. We joined in their festivities when we could, and shared with them most of our remaining provisions of food and drink. We preached to them the Good News of the Gospel, and many were converted and baptized. But after a week, our provisions were dangerously low, and we needed to obtain more. So, we continued on our journey deeper into Armenia, hoping to find traders or merchants.

"Incredibly, most of the camp of nomads decided to follow us. It wasn't just because they liked us. I think that they thought that we could help buy goods or exchange services that would be of benefit to them. They spoke a strange language among themselves, but were fluent enough in Greek and Latin to communicate with us effectively. They also added a measure of protection against bandits, who it was said, roamed in large numbers in the countryside through which we needed to travel. Altogether, our ranks swelled. I think we numbered somewhere around 114 at that time. There were about 75 men and women, in addition to the original 12 vestals and newly enlisted virgins."

"When we came upon a small village, we all tried to buy and trade for useful things, but the people bluntly shunned us. In fact, they were suspicious of us. I could see them quietly whispering something behind our backs, and motioning to others to avoid the 'outsiders'. We couldn't buy any food or trade for anything. The nomads who were with us quickly changed their attitude and started to desert us. If we weren't going to be helpful to them in obtaining goods, then we were just a hindrance, and not an aid. When three policemen showed up, the rest of the nomads disappeared in a flash.

"The chief constable asked us if there was one in our group named Hripsime. We were surprised and taken aback – we didn't expect that they would be looking for her here out on the frontier of the empire – we didn't know what to say, so we just mumbled something to the effect that we didn't understand the question. I don't think our response was convincing. There was a scurry of activity and two officers were hurriedly sent off in a certain direction. That was our cue. We all scattered in different directions, running at a good clip – but we all merged back together a mile or two outside of the village.

'Whew,' I thought, 'that was a close one. At least we managed to evade a confrontation.' We all then walked on through the night until we reached the major town of Vagharshapat.[7] This is where Sara's relatives were, or so I hoped. Not wanting to create a disturbance, we wandered about the remote outskirts until we found an old abandoned building, with a large tract of unkempt gardens surrounding it, that had once been part of a wine-making establishment – and we decided to stay there for the time being and hunker down. The garden became our new place to tend – and we spun yarn, made beads, and enjoyed the surroundings. But food was scarce and hunger was becoming more and more of a problem. We were reluctant to venture out into the city for fear of an altercation similar to what had happened in the small village."

**THE PERSECUTION**

"**AS** we later found out, the jilted Maximian was angry and upset that Hripsime had disappeared after all the wedding plans had been made. Furious, he alerted the eastern emperor Diocletian about her insubordination, and asked that if she be found, that she be returned to him at once. Diocletian then ordered his vast network of spies and investigators to track her travels, and to find her whereabouts. Rumor reached him that she might be going to Armenia, so he sent a messenger to Tiridates III, the Armenian king, to put him on guard. And Tiridates put out a notice to all the towns and villages in the region.

"Sure enough, after our ruckus in the town, word got back to King Tiridates that there was a good chance that Hripsime was in his country. When Diocletian learned of this, he urged the king to capture her and to "take care of her and send her to me." Consequently, the forces of Tiridates were on the lookout and searching everywhere they could."

"One day, we planned a covert ingress to the city to find Sara's relatives, in hope that they could help us with food and basic necessities. Five of us quietly left at night wearing dark clothing. But when we finally located them, they disavowed any knowledge of Sara, and were actually hostile toward us. They threatened to report us to the authorities. I think that Sara may have left under disagreeable conditions, and they had blotted her from their minds. Or it's possible that a change of address occurred, and these people were not relatives at all. Whatever it was, we were very disheartened. We had to leave quickly. All we could hope for is that we wouldn't be reported."

"One morning, about three months after our arrival in Vagharshapat, we awoke to find soldiers surrounding the gardens and the house. There was no movement, but they were there, and they were armed. By early afternoon, crowds of people had converged on the house – peasants and royalty both – everyone had come to see what the fuss was all about.

"Sure enough, some unscrupulous local folk had given information to the royal officials about our whereabouts. Word had gotten out that a strange group of recluses were living here, and that the young woman that was wanted by both the Roman Empire and the Kingdom of Armenia, was here. Everyone wanted to see the young Roman woman, since she was touted to be very beautiful. King Tiridates sent his servants with a golden stretcher to remove Hripsime from the house, but she resisted and they had to bring her out by force. Then, on seeing the spunk and beauty of the woman, Tiridates was overcome by lust and desire, and commanded that she be taken back to the royal palace. Gayane, Agatha, and I were permitted to accompany her.

"Hripsime was a nervous wreck. On the way to the palace, Gayane told her to endure patiently. She comforted her, reminded her of her vows, and pleaded with her not to forsake her true Bridegroom, our Lord Jesus Christ, Son of the Almighty God – and that she must not defile her virginity with a strange and unholy pagan.

"Once inside the palace, we were brought before the chair of the king.

'They tell me your name is Hripsime, or Arsema – it wasn't clear to me – but Arsema sounds more royal,' he announced. 'Nonetheless, you must know that I am in love with you, and wish for you to marry me. You will be showered with the best jewels, oils, and perfumes – your clothes will be the finest silk and velvet – and my servants will beckon to your calls and needs. You will have all the trappings of royalty at your comfort and leisure. My dear, you will want for nothing. Furthermore, your friends will be free to continue their strange way of life however they see fit. So, what do you say, my lovely Arsema?'

'But Sir, your Highness, you are already married, as I understand it,' replied Hripsime. 'Surely I could not be the driver for discord.'

'There is no issue here,' rejoined Tiridates. 'The king is free to take a second wife. I am the ultimate authority here. It is within our laws, and it is acceptable to our gods.'

'But I am a Christian. And your gods are false gods that mean nothing to me. There is only one God in the universe – and I am already betrothed to our Lord Jesus Christ, Son of the Almighty God. I cannot be a second wife. And I cannot marry a pagan. It is a sin against my God. I will never be resurrected and have eternal life in heaven.'

'Nonsense,' said the king. 'You must leave and disavow this strange unholy religion before you become totally corrupted. Accept the customs and values of my people – traditions that have guided us for eons – come over to our lifestyle and be happy – you will please the gods and help bring their benevolence upon us all.'

"Then, he grabbed Agatha and brusquely brought her to his side, saying, 'Behold, here is your mother.' Looking at Agatha, he then charged, 'Explain to your daughter the wisdom, good sense, and practicality of accepting this offer. Persuade her to re-think what she has said. Convince her to marry me and become a queen of this land.'

"Agatha just stammered and wasn't sure exactly what to say. Then, the king spoke up and said loudly, 'So, there it is.

I will give you an hour to consider my offer, while I attend to other matters. You may wait in the courtyard. When I return, I hope you will happily consent to be my queen.'

"And then we were left in the courtyard with a few guards. We were all very distraught."

"Hripsime was bitterly brooding. I could tell that she was torn with doubt and confused. Gayane continued to advise her to resist and stand firm in her faith. But Agatha was wishy-washy. There was much second-guessing and a lot of 'what if …' kind of talk. It seemed that it took forever for the hour to pass. Then, at the darkest moment, we all heard a voice from heaven that called out, saying:

*Be brave and fear not, for I am with you.*

"Then, there was no longer any fear or uncertainty. We were relieved and thankful – the decision pathway was now clear.

"In short order, an aide came to us and advised that 'the woman accede to the king's demands, for the continued health and safety of all.' We just smiled and said nothing. He had been listening to us talk, but now he left to check on the king. At that moment, there was only one guard watching us, so we seized upon the opportunity. Agatha paid a hefty sum of money for the guard to look the other way. When he did so, the four of us raced out of the courtyard and out of the palace through a little-used service door. Then we ran for miles – all the way back to the winery house, where we happily mingled with the others."

## THE HOLOCAUST

"**AFTER** a couple of hours, we were all thirsty from the chattering, so I was sent to fetch some water from the well, which was about a half mile away. I was feeling melancholy, so I walked and worked slowly. When I had filled my buckets and was returning, I saw from a distance that the path was blocked by soldiers and royal guardsmen. I looked for a way around, but couldn't find any traversable pathway. I knew I would be stopped if I tried to pass, so I just sat down, not knowing what to do.

"I was becoming more agitated and anxious by the second, and didn't want to reveal my presence, but I wanted to get as close as I could. So, I stealthily scrambled about the area looking for a way to get in without being caught – but there was nothing. It was just then that I tripped while surveying the locale and badly sprained my ankle. I fell down into a ditch behind a thick clump of rose bushes, and lay still for a while, nursing my bruise. No one saw me."

"Then, I heard a commotion as soldiers and officials rushed into the house in a frenzy of activity. Moments later, they emerged dragging Hripsime, Gayane, Agatha, and two other women into the front yard. The king was there along with his chief soldiers and bodyguards. I could hear him saying:

'Woman, why have you dared to defy your king? Why do you run and turn away? Why do you prefer the company of other women? Is that the hallmark of your despicable religion? Do you have no sense of decency? No sense of societal norms? Don't you realize that the gods could be angered?'

"Then, one of the bodyguards said, 'I heard her mother tell her to ignore the royal commands and dismiss the will of the gods. She is clearly deluded. She said that she should marry the dead son of their strange unseen god, instead.'[8]

"The king than shouted something – I couldn't make out what it was – and Agatha was seized and dragged off to the side, where she was beaten and flogged. Then the king bellowed:

'Woman, you are in need of saving – of being made right. This foul religion has possessed you and poisoned your mind. Think clearly. You can stop this senseless abuse of your mother. You can have riches and glory here with me.'

"They continued to beat Agatha, more and more severely, smashing her teeth with iron rods. With indignation, Gayane then stepped forward and reprimanded the soldiers. But, with a nod from the king, other soldiers then came forward and started to strike and hit Gayane without mercy.

"Then the king said gravely, 'Woman, what is your answer? Peace, tranquility, and happiness here with me, or conflict, harshness, and despair for the rest of your life?'

"As he was saying these words, Tiridates grew close to Hripsime, put his hands around her waist, and tried to kiss her on the cheek. Surely, she would give in to his wishes, he thought.

"But astonishingly, Hripsime pulled violently away from his embrace, tore off his scarf, knocked off his crown, and pushed him to the ground in front of his subjects. In no uncertain terms, she yelled,

> *I will not forsake my true Bridegroom, the Lord Jesus Christ, Son of the Living God. I will not renounce my faith. My God is with me now! And I will not defile myself with an unclean pagan! May God have mercy on your soul!*

"With that said, she proudly walked through the horrified crowd back to the front of the house. Everyone was staring in disbelief and amazement. The soldiers were frozen awaiting orders.

"Of course, such an indignity and embarrassment could not go unpunished. The king slowly got up, brushed himself off, and then started barking some indistinct commands. Soldiers started moving this way and that, shouting aphorisms into the air. Staff, officials, and onlookers quickly retreated away from the house. I wanted badly to go into the house with the others, but when I got up to run, my ankle collapsed and I fell down in a heap. The pain was so great, that I just lie there frozen – watching and listening as best I could."

"And that's when all hell broke loose. It was horrific. I shudder even now just to think about it. At the time, I was immobilized with fear – I couldn't move a muscle. I just lay there, paralyzed, unable to shout or cry.

"Gayane, Agatha, and two others were quickly rounded up, tortured, and killed by cutting out the tongue, slashing open the stomach, poking out the eyes, and then chopping up the body into pieces.

"Hripsime was dragged with ropes out into the backyard, where they tore out her tongue, pierced her eyes to blind her, stripped her naked, and then proceeded to hack off her arms and legs. Then, as a final insult, they severed her head with an axe.

"Then, the soldiers moved into the house and started killing everyone – men, women, virgins – young, old, it didn't matter – they killed them all with the sword, and without mercy. They bored holes in the soles of the feet of the vestals as some kind of ritual punishment, before slaying them. And I remember, there was one woman who was sick and lying in bed. She cried out to the soldiers for mercy – so, pretending to be merciful, they promptly rushed in and cut off her head with one blow. Wailing, moaning, grunting, and screaming were pervasive, but there was no defense against the onslaught. Many were simply killed by the sword while on their knees in prayer. And in this manner, everyone in our community met their death – they all received crowns of martyrdom in the kingdom of God in heaven. Altogether, I think, the number lost that day was 72 holy souls.[9]

"Witnessing all this in my half-dazed state, I could scarcely breathe – the sounds and smells were overpowering and sickening. And then I fainted, out of pain, exhaustion, and terror."

"When I awoke and came to my senses about three hours later, everything was quiet. Not a living soul was around. But the air was filled with smoke and stench, buzzards were circling, and wolves were menacing about. The soldiers had chopped up all the bodies, thrown them into a big heap, and then set them ablaze. The fire was only smoldering now, and the beasts were moving in to scavenge the remains.[10]

"I couldn't take it anymore, so methodically I picked myself up and started to limp away – pain be damned. I had nowhere to go, and didn't know where to go, so I just walked – and kept walking. Eventually, I stumbled into a municipal building and sold myself into slavery. There was just no other option. In short order, I was placed with a local law-abiding family, who gave me food and shelter, but demanded a lot of work in return. The work didn't bother me – I always did my tasks honestly – but they were very dismissive and contemptuous of my faith – always badgering and insulting me about it. I prayed for them, but my life was now just a mindless stream of humdrum existence. I had no friends or family, and there were no Christians around."

"Later, I found out that when Diocletian learned that Hripsime had been located in Armenia, but had not yet been sent back to him in Nicomedia, he sent a terse message to King Tiridates: 'Either send her back now, or marry her yourself – but do it quickly.' Of course, by then it was too late. We'll just never know how Diocletian or Maximian reacted to those dreadful events of that awful day."

## GREGORY THE ILLUMINATOR

**"I** stayed with the same couple for seven years, doing the dreary work of cooking, cleaning, and tending the garden. They treated me like a slave – which of course, I was – but there was no compassion or concern whatever for my welfare. They worshipped their gods sincerely and attended their rituals with traditional aplomb. They were always trying to get me to partake, but I always resisted. I hated the pagan worship. In turn, because of my behavior, they disrespected me even more. It was not a happy time."

"Then one day, while shopping at the local market, I heard news that perked up my ears! Everybody was talking about it, and so I listened as best I could without being conspicuous. There had been a change in the government – and in the royal family. King Tiridates had become a Christian! Holy smokes! And the royal family would soon follow. And the royal court after that. And then, who knows? The people everywhere were shocked and fearful. If the gods were angered, it could portend very bad things for the kingdom, not to mention their own lives, homes, and families. Some wanted to rebel against the king, while others wanted to fall in line solely for the purpose of ingratiating. Everyone had different fears, but I didn't hear anyone say that our God was great, and the one true God. They weren't interested in spiritual concepts like salvation, or life-after-death. They just wanted their humdrum day-to-day life to be better. And this change was worrisome to them.[11]

'How could this happen?' I wondered. "When last I saw him, he was torturing and murdering all of my friends and fellow Christians. Something significant and miraculous must have happened. And I was determined to find out what.

"The very next chance I had for a rest day, I took eagerly, and headed off to the royal palace to learn what I could. I didn't think that I would be recognized after seven years, but just to be sure, I cut my hair and wore servant's clothes. I talked with a few court laborers and they confirmed the rumor, but didn't know any details. They were only concerned with their jobs. Finally, I found a man who told me that I should talk to an individual named Gregory.[12] He was one of the Christian priests, and could usually be found in a storage room that had been turned into a makeshift chapel."

"When I went to look for Gregory in the chapel, I found a well-weathered older man who had obviously been through a lot of pain and suffering. When I told him that I was a Christian, and wanted to know what had happened to the king, he was dubious at first. But when I told him where I was born, where I lived, and everything that had happened to me, especially here in Armenia, he became really curious, and enthusiastic about learning more.

"The first chance we had, we sat down and started to relive our pasts. We soon realized that we had actually known each other as kids in Cappadocia – not buddies exactly, but as someone whom we had crossed paths with. Then he started to tell me his story – how he had come to Armenia as a young man, and gained a position as a palace official at the court of the Armenian king, Tiridates. Being a Christian, he refused to participate in the pagan religious feasts and festivals that went on. That was bad enough, but when he vocally spoke out against the beliefs and the sacred rites, he had crossed the line. Tiridates had him apprehended, tortured, and then thrown into a terrible prison, brusquely known as the 'pit of oblivion'." [13]

**Khosrovidukht**

"After Gregory had spent 13 years 'in the pit', he was given a miraculous lifeline by, of all people, Tiridates' sister Khosrovidukht.

"It turns out that after the horrible events of that day at the winery house, King Tiridates suffered terrible spells of delusion and paranoia. He was possessed by Satan, the devil, and believed that he had been changed into a wild boar [14]– it drove him to madness and he simply lost his sanity. He would aimlessly wander around in the forest, adopting the behavior of a wild beast. I think it was God's punishment for his actions at the winery house. In addition, his soldiers were beset by devils, and began to act like wild animals, running through the forests, gnawing at themselves, and tearing their clothes. Khosrovidukht did everything she possibly could to bring her brother back to sanity, but nothing worked.

"Then, one night in her sleep, Khosrovidukht had a dream where a vision from God appeared to her. She saw a man in the likeness of a bright shining light coming towards her – an angel – and he said to her:

> *There is no other cure for these torments that have come upon your brother, unless you send to the city of Artashat and bring here the prisoner Gregory. When he comes, he will teach you the remedy.*

"Khosrovidukht had this vision five times. But when she spoke of her visions to the officials at court, they mocked her, saying, 'You too have gone mad. It's not possible that this man is still alive after 13 years. No one lives that long in "the pit". He probably dropped dead the first week he was there, if not from the stench, then from the snakes. If you tell the king about this vision, he'll surely think you are mentally deranged. Who knows what he might do to you!'

"However, some of the underground Christians advised her to report it to the king immediately – else she would suffer great torments herself, and the king would become even worse. Now, Khosrovidukht was raised in the Zoroastrian religion, but had secretly adopted Christianity, along with her sister-in-law Ashkhen (who was the Queen), through the efforts of the Armenian Christian underground.[15] She was of a mild disposition, and secretly helped protect the Christian community from religious persecution. But now, she wasn't sure what to do. She was nervous, hesitant, and fearful.

"However, after careful deliberation, she decided to tell her brother about her dreams, and then just let events play out as they may. And so, that is what she did. And thank God, the king reacted normally.

"Straight away, Tiridates dispatched Khosrovidukht's foster father Awtay to the castle of Artashat in order to release Gregory out of the dungeon and deep pit. When Gregory was brought to the king, he was malnourished and emaciated, but alive. The odds of him having been alive were slim, but I'm told that he had been secretly fed during his captivity by the underground Christians, possibly even Ashkhen and Khosrovidukht, on occasion." [16]

## The Conversion of King Tiridates

"Gregory convinced the king of the great power of God, and managed to get him to cry out, 'By the power of the god of Gregory,[17] his holy son, and all his holy angels,[18] I believe in you, and ask that you purge away this affliction that ails me.' With similar words of his own, Gregory expunged the demons in the name of Jesus Christ,[19] our Lord and Savior, in such a manner that Tiridates proclaimed his belief, and asked for conversion on the spot. Gregory explained to him that one of his acts of penance must be to venerate the remains of the holy martyr Hripsime, and the king consented. Within a few days, the king and the royal family were baptized by Gregory in a royal ceremony,[20] and plans were in the works to convert and baptize the entire royal court.[21]

"King Tiridates repented for his sins, and had the ashes and lingering remains of the holy martyrs laid in a holy place until such time that a chapel could be built over the relics. And he wanted to keep alive for all eternity the name of the beautiful maiden, who had never compromised her faith and sacrificed her life for it. So, he ordered a spectacular temple to be built in Hripsime's name." [22]

"Gregory had great hope for the future of the country and was excited about spreading the Gospel,[23] building churches, and saving souls.[24] 'There is so much yet to do,' he would say.[25] I felt invigorated just being in his presence.

"I too, felt that changes were in the air. I could foresee God doing great things in the country. I became so enamored with Gregory's ministry, that I had to re-examine my own life and mission. My quest to go to Iberia had been twice thwarted, but now I felt a renewed sense of vigor. My life mired in slavery had to change. I had to return to my original mission. I had to bring the faith to Iberia. And I had to go now!

"When I told Gregory about my calling, and my current predicament, he said that he could make arrangements for a trustworthy Christian royal official to accompany me on travel close to the border, but at that point I would be on my own. The official would not be able to enter the foreign land and would have to return to court. He was concerned about my welfare, but could see the determination in my eyes – he knew that it was my destiny. Of course, I eagerly embraced the idea and warmly accepted the assistance.

"Within a week, the arrangements had been made, I had

secretly gathered all my things together, and quietly found the right time to slip out of my master's house and make my way to the palace. I met up with Gregory and the escort, and we immediately set out on the road. We knew that a 'runaway slave' declaration would be forthcoming, so we had to move fast. I tied the grapevine cross in my hair, grabbed my duffel, and off we went."

## ON THE WAY TO IBERIA

"**GREGORY** left us at the city limit and I continued on with the escort into the countryside. We walked for days, sometimes getting lifts on donkeys or carriages. When we came to a town or village with a public square, I would preach the Good News if the opportunity presented itself. Many people listened, and a few converted, but there was always many hoots and catcalls. My escort did an honorable job of whisking me away when things looked worrisome. But I was happy to have the opportunity to praise God. We had a little money, but we tried to be as frugal as possible, living by the grace of God, and sometimes on the gifts of strangers.

"The trip was very wearisome and my legs kept getting heavier and heavier. Conflicting thoughts of what I was doing and where I was going kept swirling around in my mind: 'Can I do this alone? Can I put up with the ridicule and scorn? Can I defend myself against verbal and physical attacks? Is this task even possible for a "nobody" like myself?' I staunchly refused to give in and call it quits, but the constant second-guessing wore me out. At one point, I was so exhausted, and a bit discouraged from my less-than-stellar evangelism, that I collapsed under a shady tree, and fell fast asleep.

"There and then I had a vision – a vision of a majestic

man bathed in white light – like an angel – who silently walked up to me, smiled, and handed me a scroll on which was written 10 motivating proverbs inspired from the Holy Scriptures. When I awoke, the scroll was miraculously in my hands, and I was elated – I was filled with emotional joy and encouraged to get up fresh and continue on my mission. As we walked, I memorized the sayings and kept repeating them over and over in my head.

"That scroll has been ever always with me. You may keep it as a treasure, along with my grapevine cross, to remind you of me, and help you in your quest to spread the Gospel of our Lord. My dearest friends, listen to His words and feel the presence of God:

> 'Go and teach the people of all nations, baptizing them in the name of the Father, and of the Son, and of the Holy Spirit'.[26]
>
> 'Do not be afraid. Go and tell the Good News to all'.[27]
>
> 'Teach them to observe all things that I have taught you; Remember, I am with you always, even to the end of the world'.[28]
>
> 'You have seen My glory – a light that reveals My will, and can bring salvation to all the people'.[29]
>
> 'Don't worry about saying the right thing – the Holy Spirit will teach you at the proper time just what to say'.[30]
>
> 'I will give you the words and wisdom, such that none of your enemies will be able to refute or contradict you'.[31]
>
> 'Whoever welcomes you welcomes Me; and whoever welcomes Me welcomes the One who sent Me'.[32]
>
> 'There is no difference between slave and free, or between male and female; all are one in the eyes of God'.[33]
>
> 'Wherever the Gospel is preached, this woman will be remembered for what she has done'.[34]
>
> 'Worry not about those who can destroy your body but not your soul – rather, revere your God, who can destroy both your body and your soul'.[35]

"A few days later, in the early morning, we reached a point close to the border with Iberia. It was along a mountain ridge line that overlooked a picturesque valley. It looked like sheep were grazing in the valley below. My guide and escort graciously bid his farewell, and with a respectful wish for good luck, turned around and retreated back along the way we had come.

"I was on my own, and ready or not, I was entering Iberia. My calling and my true mission in life was now beginning."

## NOTES

---

1. It was during the episcopacy of Bishop Alexander of Alexandria (312-328 AD) that the Arian heresy reached its height.

2. The port of arrival was actually Seleucia Pieria, the working port for Syrian Antioch. The city was about 10 miles away.

3. Actually, the caravan headed northeast.

4. The northern end of Mesopotamia was called various names at different times, including Galatia, Pontica (Pontus), Cappadocia, Commagene, and Armenia.

5. At the time, Edessa was outside the border of the Kingdom of Armenia, but within the general region known as 'Greater Armenia'. The region had first been evangelized by the disciple Thaddaeus, one of the 70 who had been sent by the Apostle Thomas after the resurrection (Thaddaeus, one of the 12 apostles, is often indistinguishable from Thaddaeus of Edessa, one of the 70 disciples). He healed King Abgarus of a serious malady and preached to all the people in the court. The royal embracing of Christianity continued until King Abgar VIII was baptized around 180 AD (evidenced by coins issued between 180 and 192, showing a cross on the headdress of the king). Records say that a man named Palut was made bishop of Edessa by Serapion of Antioch in 190 AD. About this time, an account of Saint Thomas' mission to India appears in Syriac literature, entitled "The Acts of Judas Thomas". It contains 'The Hymn of the Soul', considered the gem of Syriac literature, and ends with the apostle's martyrdom, and the bringing back of his bones to Edessa.

An interesting story in reputable historical records (Reference: "The Epistles of Jesus Christ and Abgarus, King of Edessa", in Eusebius, "Church History", in *Nicene and Post-Nicene Fathers of the Christian Church*, vol. 1, trans. by Arthur Cushman McGiffert, ed. by Philip Schaff and Henry Wace [Grand Rapids, MI: William. B. Eerdmans, 1982]) is the correspondence between King Abgarus and Jesus. Abgarus had heard about the healing miracles of Jesus, and asked him to come to Edessa to assist in his own healing, since he had a terminal illness. He wrote: "For I hear the Jews ridicule you, and intend you mischief. My city is indeed small, but neat, and large enough for us both." A footman named Ananias personally delivered the letter, wrote an answer dictated by Jesus, and delivered the reply back to King Abgarus. Jesus' message was: "I must inform you, that I must fulfill all the ends of my mission in this country, and after that be received up again to him who sent me. But after my ascension, I will send one of my disciples, who will cure your disease, and give life to you, and all that are with you." Indeed, Edessa was one of the first places visited by the evangelists.

6. an encampment of nomads, colloquially called a 'gypsy camp'

7. Vagharshapat is now the largest satellite city of the capital Yerevan, the fourth largest city in Armenia, and the most populous municipal community in Armavir province. It is also known as 'Echmiadzin (Ejmiatsin)', after Christianity became the state religion in Armenia. The city's oldest name was Artimed, derived from the ancient Greek god Artemis, and it was partly settled by Jewish captives. From 120 to 330 AD, it was capital of the Arsacid kingdom of Armenia, the family dynasty from which came King Tiridates III.

8. The bodyguard didn't really know who said these things. He just figured that it made a more engaging story by saying that it was the mother.

9. Estimates of the breakdown vary, but a good guess would be about 18 men, 27 women, 15 virgins, and the 12 original vestal virgins.

10. The entire story of the persecution against the virgin ascetic community is recorded by Moses of Khoran in *The History of the Armenians*, written approximately 440 AD.

11. For the ordinary layperson, besides the obvious replacement of traditional gods and pagan temples, there were social changes that would affect them. One notable area was marriage – the Christian church formalized the institution and made it necessary for the couple to legalize their union through the swearing of vows, which adhered to the Christian doctrine. Choice of partner was more limited, as partners now had to come from outside one's family. Polygamy was prohibited. Some traditional rituals were now forbidden, such as mourning rites where the mourners ritualistically cut their faces and arms. The Christian church also brought benefits, such as setting up hospitals, clinics, and orphanages for the poor, sick, and disadvantaged.

12. also known as Grigor Lusavorich

13. Khor-Virap prison at Artashat was known as the 'pit of oblivion', because the rumor was that nobody ever returned from that dreadful place.

14. It was said that Tiridates suffered from lycanthropy – the belief that one is transformed into a wolf or other animal.

15. Christian converts had quietly existed in Armenia for over two centuries, following the first missionary visits from the apostles Thaddeus and Bartholomew. It was a major underground center of the faith.

16. From this time onwards, Khosrovidukht and her family dedicated the rest of their lives to the service of Jesus Christ. As King Tiridates III encouraged and supported the spread of Christianity, Khosrovidukht and Ashkhen participated in the planning and initial construction of the Echmiadzin Cathedral, Saint Gayane Church, and Saint Hripsime Church. During the construction of these churches, Ashkhen and Khosrovidukht donated their royal jewels to help with the expenses.

17. Many newly converted pagans did not fully understand the nature of the one true God, especially if the conversion was the result of a 'miracle'. They simply, and naively, called Him "the God of Nino" or "the God of Gregory", or "the God of 'whoever was the miracle-worker' ".

18. Tiridates did not yet fully comprehend the true essence of the Triune God of Christianity. So, in his quotation, the words representing divinity are not capitalized.

19. an early example of exorcism

20. By the time Nino had conversed with Gregory, the information she had previously received was already outdated. The royal family had already been converted just days earlier. Gregory would go on to baptize all the royal court, and then the entire army (in the Euphrates river, according to legend).

21. Persuaded by the power of the cure, at some point, King Tiridates proclaimed Christianity as the official religion of the state in Armenia. Scholars differ on the exact date of this – some say as early as 301 AD, while others say that 314 AD is more likely. Thus, it's possible that Armenia became the first nation in the world to officially adopt Christianity.

For the record, historians suggest that King Tiridates may well have adopted Christianity for more practical reasons, rather than a change of faith based on his miraculous recovery of health. The end of the ancient pagan religion was a fine excuse to confiscate the old temple treasuries which were jealously guarded by a hereditary class of priests. The religion was also a useful point of distinction between Armenia and Sasanid Persia, which had been trying to spread Zoroastrianism (which focused on the worship of Mithra and a pantheon of lesser gods) in the country. Christianity, therefore, became a means to resist Persian cultural imperialism.

22. The Temple of Hripsime was eventually erected on the very site where she was killed. Today, St. Hripsime Church in Echmiadzin is dedicated to her. The current structure was consecrated in 618 AD, and contains her tomb in the catacombs beneath the building. According to legend, the exact spot for the shrine was pinpointed by a shaft of light that descended from heaven – and then Jesus Christ struck the ground with a golden hammer until the earth shook.

23. King Tiridates issued a decree by which he granted Gregory full rights to begin carrying out the conversion of the entire nation to the Christian faith.

24. Christianity soon became the official state religion of the Armenian Nation. Gregory was then made the first bishop in Armenia's history, and he set about formally establishing the Christian Church. To get the ball rolling, Tiridates gave Gregory some 15 provinces (or so) worth of territory to establish the Armenian Church. The old pagan temples were torn down, and the whole nation was obliged to embrace the new faith. Churches and monasteries sprang up everywhere, and the Armenian aristocracy quickly followed the royal family's example with many noble families converting to Christianity.

Gregory had state backing to spread the Gospel message, and it was a work continued by his descendants who inherited his role of first bishop of Armenia. Gregory used two powerful tools to spread the word: education and military power. Schools were established in which children of the existing pagan priestly class were prepared for the Christian priesthood. Meanwhile, military units were dispatched to destroy pagan temple sites and confiscate their vast riches, which were then used to fund Christian building projects. Naturally, many temple sites, along with several rich and semi-independent feudal principalities, resisted the new policy, and those were met with force. Pagan traditions were never fully eradicated, but they certainly became weakened by the removal of the temples and their economic resources. Still, many anti-Christian and pro-Persian aristocratic families persisted in resisting at least into the next century. Gregory, meanwhile, oversaw mass baptisms, and bishops and priests were appointed to guide the ever-growing flock of faithful. Reference: M. Cartwright, "Saint Gregory the Illuminator", *World History Encyclopedia*, February 2018.

25. Some records indicate that Gregory would later go on to convert King Umayr of Caucasian Albania (see map in Appendix), but some scholars believe that this was actually done by one of his descendants, also named Gregory.

26. Compare with Matthew 28:19.

27. Compare with Matthew 28:10.

28. Compare with Matthew 28:20.

29. Compare with Luke 2:32.

30. Compare with Luke 12:11-12.

31. Compare with Luke 21:15.

32. Compare with Matthew 10:40 and John 13:20.

33. Compare with Galatians 3:28.

34. Compare with Matthew 26:13.

35. Compare with Matthew 10:28 and Luke 12:4.

# 5 IBERIA – THE EARLY YEARS

*Be not afraid to reach out and preach to the pagans of this region – for I will be by your side – and you will have My blessing.*

**THE SETTING:** On her deathbed, Nino is relating her life story to her friends Salome and Perozhavra.

**THE STORY LINE:** Nino has crossed the border into Iberia with little more than her cross and her scroll, and is determined to bring the Gospel to the people of this land. But hardships and ordeals are in the works.

## INTO IBERIA

"**EARLY** in the morning, I crossed the border into Iberia carrying my cross, my scroll, and a small duffel bag. I remember that it was unseasonably cold. But it got warmer as I descended into the valley. As I got closer to the sheep, they became agitated and started moving around and making funny noises. Naturally, this woke up the shepherds, and they scurried forth to see what the commotion was about. When they first saw me from a distance, they thought that I was a rustler – one who was trying to steal their animals. They shouted something – a warning, I guess – but I just kept walking towards them. I hollered a 'Hello', but they didn't seem to understand me.

"The shepherds' anxiety was abated when I got closer

and they could see that I was not a thief or a robber. I greeted them as best I could – although the language was a bit of a barrier – and they seemed to be friendly. Then, I told them who I was, why I had come, and showed them my cross and scroll. But they had trouble believing and understanding just what I was doing there. Actually, they weren't much for any religion or god-fearing – they were just country peasants, concerned mostly with the welfare of their flocks and families. But they were just astounded that a woman would have traveled over the mountain all by herself during the night.[1] Such a thing wasn't heard of for an everyday person – they just assumed that I had to be a runaway slave.

"But I was a foreigner and there was no jurisdiction here. So, they were happy – and also impatient – to bring me to their homes and their families. They assumed I needed feeding and bathing, and one of the families would certainly be able to see to it. So, two of the shepherds walked with me back to their village, called Akhalkalaki, which was near a beautiful blue lake,[2] while the others stayed to tend the sheep.

"Since I had no family, no owner, and no contacts here whatsoever, I was considered to be a 'captive' – not a slave, but more like a prize, or a spoil-of-war. As a 'captive', I was basically a servant, but was treated much kindlier than a slave – and with more respect. One of the families graciously let me stay with them, so I had food and shelter – of course, I was expected to do my share of the chores – which I did without any complaint. I was on good relations with the villagers – tending to, comforting, and healing some of the sick with my prayers. I won their respect but not their hearts, however, which discouraged me a great deal."

## THE FIRST MIRACLES

"**THEN**, one day, when I was quietly cultivating the garden, I heard the Voice of God speak to me:

> *Be not afraid to reach out and preach to the pagans of this region – for I will be by your side – and you will have My blessing.*

"My faith had not been much of an issue. I had constructed a small cross in the center of the village, where I would sometimes stop and pray, but no one took notice. In fact, they rarely paid any attention to the pagan religious customs either, and showed little interest in mine – but two or three times a year, they were obliged to attend a state-sponsored festival to worship the local gods. The intent was to please the gods, so that they would bring good fortune to the nation and the people – good weather, good crops, good babies, etc. I had no desire to attend – I bowed out twice, making up some lame excuse, but the third time was a bigger celebration. Nearly everyone in the village was going on a pilgrimage to the nearby city of Mtskheta to venerate the pagan gods Armazi and Zaden.[3] It was a big deal. They intimated that I really had to go, so I reluctantly tagged along with the group of villager-pilgrims."

### The Ceremony in Mtskheta

"After a long day's walk, we arrived in Mtskheta at the ceremony grounds. The worship ritual had just begun – and it was very eerie and disheartening. A large crowd of people, including the king and the royal court, stood in solemn reverence before their gods, trembling with nervous anticipation, while the priests made preparations for the offering of blood sacrifices. Finally, when the incense was burned, the sacrificial blood poured out, and the trumpets and cymbals resounded, the king and all the people prostrated themselves before the lifeless statues in senseless obedience.

"When I saw this, I became overwhelmed with pity, sorrow, indignation, and a zeal to show them the real truth about God, heaven, and salvation. My heart pounded, my hands shook, and my body burned with fire. Sighing from the depths of my soul, my eyes filled with tears as I looked up to heaven, and began to pray:

> *Almighty God! By Your great mercy, bring these people to the knowledge of Yourself, the One, true and holy God. I ask You to scatter these idols as the wind blows dust and ashes from the face of the earth. Look down with mercy upon these people, whom You have created with Your almighty hand, and whom You have honored with Your divine image! O Lord and Master, You did so love Your creation that You sacrificed Your Only-begotten Son for the salvation of a fallen humanity – I beg You to deliver the souls of these people away from the destructive power of Satan – the prince of darkness – who has blinded their eyes of understanding, so that they do not see the true path to salvation. O Lord, grant that I may see the final destruction of the idols standing here so proudly. My God, I pray that this nation, and even every person on the earth, might be brought to understand and appreciate the gift of salvation given by You – and that all nations and all people might worship You, the One Eternal God, and Your Only-begotten Son, our Lord Jesus Christ, to Whom belongs glory and honor forever.*

"Although my words were vocalized, they were very quiet, and no one could hear me. A few moments passed. And then, suddenly the sky darkened, the temperature dropped, a violent wind began to blow, tremendous thunder and lightning ensued, and torrents of giant hailstones fell from the sky – shattering the pagan statues and smashing the temple. The immense statue of Armazi was utterly destroyed by the storm, and came tumbling down in a heap of debris. The terrified worshipers fled, scattering across the city. A mighty downpour of rain followed, and washed all the broken pieces of the idols into the river and out of sight.

"I witnessed this event, and knew that it had been in answer to my anguished prayer. I thanked God ever so gratefully, and in humble appreciation, joined back up with the frightened villagers. The people were wet and despondent, but I was wet and elated. I knew that God was with me."

"On the way back to the village, the group decided to stop in the town of Urbnisi,[4] to rest, dry out, and get something to eat. While everyone was recuperating, I began thinking – and realized that my future lay back in Mtskheta – in the city, where the culture and philosophy were greatest – where the rule of royalty was centered – and where I might be able to make a bigger difference.

"And so, I asked my custodian for my release, explaining to him my desire to stay in Urbnisi, and then later return to Mtskheta. I paid him some money, and he agreed. He was a good man, although I don't think he understood what really drove me. Shortly thereafter, the group of plucky pilgrims got up and began their trek back to the village of Akhalkalaki, while I stayed behind in Urbnisi. I got a small room in a boarding house and settled in."

### Healing the Pagan's Sick Child

"I worked some odd-jobs for people, but mostly I tried to provide comfort and healing to anyone who seemed to need it. At the same time, I would always try to speak about my holy and loving God – the one true God – and the wonders of His Kingdom in heaven. Sometimes, I was met with indifference, sometimes with disdain, and sometimes with curiosity. But I wasn't fazed – I wouldn't relent. The word quickly got out that I could help the sick and the unhappy."

"One day, out of the blue, a desperate mother came to my home and asked if I could do anything that would heal her sick child, who was slowly dying in her arms. As was the practice among the people of the city, that when a child fell seriously ill and couldn't be cured by the doctors, the mother would take him door-to-door asking the neighbors for their folk remedies or homespun cures. The doctors had thrown up their hands, and she had taken the boy to many homes, but no one had been able to help him – and she was afraid that he would die very soon. This woman was at her wit's end. She was a hardened pagan who detested the Christian faith, and had even tried to prevent other people from coming to me. But as a last resort, when all other options had been exhausted, she came to me begging.

"When I saw the young child, I immediately felt a sense of connection between him, myself, and God. I placed my hair shawl on him, and holding my cross and scroll, prayed to Almighty God:

> *O God, creator of all things and controller of all that happens, I pray to you for the welfare of this innocent child. He is in Your image, but is very young, and has not yet been familiarized with sin. I pray that You restore him to health, so that he can serve You in this life and the next. In Jesus' name, I ask that You cast away the illness in this boy. In the name of my Lord, Jesus Christ, hear now Your humble servant. In Jesus' Name - In Jesus' Name - Amen.*

"And then, at the sound of our Savior's name, a smile played on the lips of the little one, and he miraculously recovered. The mother was overjoyed at the return of her son, but she would not listen to my preaching. I think she considered me a sorceress – a daughter of the god Armazi.

However, she did spread the word throughout the land, that I was a 'great healer'.

"I was sad for her and happy at the same time – sad, because she wouldn't receive the Word of God – but happy because the young boy was better, and she was cheerful again. Who knows? Maybe that boy will someday become a great Christian leader." [5]

"I only stayed in Urbnisi for about three months; then, my money had run out. So, with just the clothes on my back, a small duffel, my cross, and my scroll, I decided to return to Mtskheta and follow my calling. On the outskirts of the city, on a cliff that overlooked the palace and markets, I built a wooden cross, in remembrance of when the idols were dispersed, and in anticipation of a grand Christian awakening.[6] It was an emotional moment, and I cried for a long time."

## THE ROYAL GARDENS

"**I** had no place to stay, so I headed for the royal palace, hoping to find work as a servant of some kind. As I was walking through the gardens, which surrounded the complex, I stumbled upon a laborer and we started talking.

'Are you lost?' he asked quizzically.

'I'm looking for the official in charge of the servants,' I said. 'I'm in need of a place to stay and I'm hoping to find a job here.'

'Well, I'm afraid you might be disappointed,' said the worker. 'With all the disruptions due to this dumb religious thing, I don't think that they're hiring much. What are your skills anyway?'

'I can do all the domestic services, cooking, cleaning, gardening, …'

'Aha – gardening, did you say? I don't suppose you

know anything about rose bushes?'

'In fact, I do. I know when and how to trim – how to water and how to feed, and …'[7]

'Excellent,' he interrupted. 'It just so happens that I'm the royal gardener, and I'm in need of an assistant – spring is here, things are growing like crazy, my wife is not as able as she once was, and my trainee has just left town. When can you start?'

'I first have to find a place to stay.'

'No problem,' said the head gardener. 'You can stay in the hut my trainee used. With a little sprucing up, it will be just fine.'

"And so, that very day, I became the assistant to the royal gardener. His name was Levan, and we soon became close friends. I made my home in a tent hut beneath an overgrown, but stylishly trimmed, bramble bush in the garden of the king. The royal gardener and his wife lived in a nearby hut. I did all of the gardening tasks asked of me, and it was very satisfying tending to god's magnificent creation. In the evening, I quietly prayed to God, and reflected on His holy Word.

"Levan and I would often have long talks about things – all sorts of different things. He learned that I was a Christian, and asked about my cross and my scroll. He was a pagan himself, but not religious. He was interested in my faith and listened attentively to my ramblings."

**A Birth in Answer to Prayers**

"One day, during the course of our chatting, he mentioned that his life was still unfulfilled because he and his wife, Anastasia, had not been able to conceive a child. He had heard of my healing ability, and asked if there was anything that I could do. So, there and then, in the middle of the rose garden, in the middle of the day, I prayed for a child to be born to the gardener and his wife – and he joined me in the prayer. That night, I prayed again – and continued to pray every night.

"After two months or so, Levan told me that Anastasia was pregnant. He was very happy and excited. He walked with a crisper step and occasionally joined me in evening prayers. After nine months, God granted them a beautiful and healthy baby boy, and we all rejoiced exceedingly. For the next six months, Levan had to help care for the infant, so I had to pull double duty in tending to the gardens – but I didn't mind at all – I was happy for them. They named him Davit, and affectionately called him Dato.

"Then, one day, another wonderful event occurred. Levan and Anastasia came to me and asked if they could be converted to my God – the god of the Christians. They were convinced that it was through my prayers, and my God, that the pregnancy and birth had been successful – they wanted to show their respect and give their thanks – and they wanted a new Light in their life – the Light and Love of Christ Jesus, both for their future and to help guide the future upbringing of their child. I was thrilled and delighted.

"That very day, we went to the fountain in the middle of the gardens, and I baptized Levan, Anastasia, and Davit in the Name of the Father, and of the Son, and of the Holy Spirit. They were elated to start a new chapter in their lives. They promised to be good Christian parents, raise their child with good Christian values, and earnestly spread the Good News of Jesus Christ whenever and wherever they could. It was a very special and moving occasion. And I tell you sincerely, that to this very day, that couple have remained true to their word. They have helped me in many, many ways in my missionary efforts."

## The Healing and Conversion of Queen Nana

"A few months later, I received a message that I had been summoned by the queen – Queen Nana. Being a lowly groundskeeper, I was somewhat surprised, but I dutifully reported to the queen's chambers. The furnishings were lavish, but pictures and statues of idols were everywhere – I shuddered at the sights. Looking tired, the queen was resting on a cushioned bench, and she motioned for me to come forward.

'You are the runaway slave girl from Armenia, the captiva named Nino?' she asked.

'I am, your highness.'

'You have gained a reputation for holiness, because of your daily piety, your good works, and your miraculous healings. While I do not understand the gods you worship – living a very devout life of sobriety and virtue – I know that you are close to your gods, and that they listen when you talk to them. I've heard that you can even command them to do things – healing the sick being one of those things.

'My dear, that is why I have called you here today. You see, I am dying from this cursed ailment that afflicts me day and night.[8] The doctors are at a loss – they can do nothing. And the priests have given me all the potions and made all the proper sacrifices to the gods – but I am uncured. I think they are punishing me for something, but I don't know what. I was hoping that your gods might be able to pinpoint the error of my ways, and then this sickness would pass away. Of course, you will be rewarded, and I will be forever grateful.'

"To which I replied, 'Your royal highness, you must be able to think beyond your upbringing and your traditions – beyond your way of worship – beyond your gods and idols. Their time has passed – their influence is ended. They are unreal and obsolete – invented and illusory – and relics of a bygone era. You must be able to embrace the Good News – the New Way – and accept the One and Only God Almighty, and His Only begotten Son, Jesus Christ, through whom you can be saved, and live forever. It is the only way – all other paths lead to destruction and eternal damnation. If you can do this, then He will heal you of your afflictions, and give you joy and happiness. That alone would be my reward.'

'My dear, that is a lot to swallow. Can't you just talk to your god on my behalf, like you have done for all the others?'

'Your highness, I have no authority in this palace of pagan idols. My seat of authority resides in the places pleasing to my God – the one and only true God – where His glory is proclaimed and where praise to Him is manifest. There is no higher authority than my Lord Jesus Christ, to whom this humble captive woman loves and obeys above all others. I cannot do anything here in this den of iniquity. But, if you come to my humble tent, release all your preconceived notions, traditions, and beliefs, and put all your faith in the Good News of Jesus Christ, then you will surely be healed by the grace of His power, and receive salvation and eternal life.

'And so, my Lady, that is simply the way that it is. If there is nothing else, then I will take my leave of you.'

"Queen Nana just looked at me and didn't say anything. I bowed and slowly walked away.

"With that, I returned to my hut and went back to my daily chores. I didn't know what to expect – punishment, sacking; it could have been anything. When I told Levan of this, he was not optimistic. Nevertheless, I did not regret my actions, and was determined to live with whatever the consequences were."

"The next day, in the late afternoon, Queen Nana came

to my humble abode, accompanied by two attendants and two slaves. She had to be carried into my tent because of her ailments. When she was comfortably set and contented, she said to me:

'Nino, I have thought about everything you have said. And I am ready to reject all that has come before, and accept all that will come with the New Way. I put my future in your hands.'

"And to that I replied, 'Then I will bring to you this oil and this basin of water, and I will give you my blessings. Prepare yourself for the sacrament – I will prompt you on what to say – bow your head, clasp your hands together, and close your eyes. My hand will lay on your shoulder, and I will anoint your head three times with the water of eternal life.'[9] And then, after a moment of silent introspection, I said to her:

'Do you believe in the one true God, the Father Almighty, creator of heaven and earth?'

'Yes, I do.'

'Do you believe in our Lord and Savior Jesus Christ, His Only-begotten Son, with all of your heart, all of your mind, and all of your soul?'

'Yes, I do.'

'Do you believe in the Holy Spirit, the holy Christian church, the forgiveness of sins, the resurrection of the body, and life everlasting?'[10]

'Yes, I do.'

'Then by the power and grace of God, I baptize you in the Name of the Father, and of the Son, and of the Holy Spirit. Open your eyes, and look up to the sky. In Jesus' Name, may the Almighty Spirit come upon you and give you peace and new life. In Jesus' Name, stand up, be healed, and give thanks to God!'

"And then Queen Nana bravely stood up, and was

absolutely radiant in the fading light. Her face was flushed with color, she took deep breaths, and tears flowed down her cheeks – and then she was overcome with emotion, and fell prostrate on the floor in prayer. Years of doubt, alienation, and suffering came miraculously out of her in a torrent of supplication. Her penitence was genuine and her conversion was glorious. Her illness and her demons had departed her, and she was born anew.

"She spent the next hour praising and thanking God – promising to follow the Christian path and to bring others into the faith. She was like a new person in every respect. And I joined with her in thanking God and praising His holy Name."

"Now, it so happened that the two servants who had accompanied the queen, a Jewish priest and his daughter Abiathar, witnessed the queen's physical and spiritual transformation, and were enthralled by the miracle. Awestruck by the power of God, they fell to their knees and asked me for forgiveness. When I explained to them that I was just a conduit for the miraculous works of God, they slowly began to understand, and asked if they, too, could be converted and receive the sacrament of baptism. They had never heard of Jesus of Nazareth and knew little about the Christian movement. So, of course, I obliged and gave a long-winded explanation – probably too long, in retrospect – of the Passion of Christ and the early Christian church. They were mesmerized by it all, and I gave much thanks to God. Then, I gave them the sacrament of baptism, just as I had done for Queen Nana. The queen witnessed the rite, and by the end of the evening, we were all joyfully praising God and communing in mutual fellowship. There was no rich or poor, noble or servant, male or female. We were all equal in our love for God – and equal in God's love for us. All in all, it was a remarkable evening; one that I will never forget.

"When I told Levan about this the next morning, all he could say was, 'The king is not going to be happy.' I didn't care."

*****

The telling of Nino's life story is interrupted here, as she directly engages Salome and Perozhavra in friendly discourse:

"It was shortly afterwards, I believe, when I first met you, my dear Perozhavra."

"Yes," said Perozhavra. "I am originally from Sivnia, but was betrothed to the ruler of the Kartli region. I heard about your miraculous cure of the pagan woman's young son almost immediately, since Urbnisi is in that region. I talked to many of the people, and learned about this foreign runaway slave woman, who professed a strange religion, and was healing people of many illnesses. People swore by their accounts and I was very intrigued and wanted to meet you personally. But, by the time I got around to actually going to your house, you had already left for Mtskheta. So, I sent a message to the queen in Mtskheta, telling her everything I knew about you.

"A few months later, I got a letter back from Queen Nana, telling me all about you, her miraculous recovery from her illness, and her conversion to your religion, the religion of the Christians. She invited me to come to the royal palace, where we could get together and learn more about the ways of the Christ. Of course, I jumped at the opportunity, and came as soon as I could. It was shortly thereafter that we met for the first time, and shared in the fellowship of Christ."

"Yes, I remember, you converted and were baptized in a beautiful ceremony."

"One that I will never forget. And for that I am ever grateful, and at your service. You taught me how to pray, how to fast, and about doing good works. I am your disciple, and will do whatever I can to help you spread the Word."

"And your help is crucial to saving souls and bringing the Good News to all the people. You have already helped me tremendously, and I hope your work will continue long after I am gone."

"Shhh," said Perozhavra. "Don't talk like that."

"And my dear Salome ... – it was a few years later that I met you for the first time. Back then, your name was Beoun, a very pretty name."

"Yes," said Salome. "I was originally from Armenia, but came to Iberia as an intercultural exchange <wink, wink> to marry Rev II, the son of King Mirian and Queen Nana.[11] They changed my name to Salome – more politically correct, I guess.[12] I learned about you from Queen Nana shortly after I arrived, and was keen on meeting you. I was a follower of Zoroaster, but_when I first came to one of your prayer meetings, I was blown away, and just had to learn more. So, I continued to come, and engage in fellowship with you and Nana, Perozhavra, and sometimes Levan and Anastasia, Abiathar, and a few others. I was taken in by your knowledge and friendliness, your grace and charm – and of course, the appeal of the message; and it wasn't long before I knew that I had to convert and accept Christ as my personal Savior. You baptized me – Nana and Perozhavra were there – and it was all very beautiful. That day, I became your disciple, and like Perozhavra, will do whatever I can to help you spread the Word."

"You are so dear to me, my two friends, I love you so

much. Although I may remain ever close to you, most people will soon forget me – I'm just a minor footnote in a much bigger chronicle. But the work we do here – and I hope you always continue – is the most important work of all – bringing people to see the Light, receive the Spirit, and understand the Word. The stakes are the future salvation and eternal life in heaven of thousands and thousands of people. They must be made aware of the Good News of our Lord Jesus Christ. The cost to us may be high on this earth, but the rewards in heaven will be the most blissful imaginable. We are proud and privileged to serve the Lord. There can be no greater undertaking."[13]

"Amen," said all three together.

Nino continues here the telling of her life story:

*****

"When Queen Nana extolled her new faith to King Mirian, an ardent pagan, he paid her no attention, although she mentioned it to him often. He became well aware of his wife's religious conversion, but was intolerant of her new faith. He reiterated the official policy of persecuting Christians, even threatening to divorce his wife if she didn't leave the faith. Even so, my preaching, healing, and fellowship gradually began to make an impression on the royal court – noble and commoner alike – and I don't think the king was too happy. He was unwilling to let go of his pagan beliefs, despite his wife's miraculous recovery and embracing of the new religion. And he didn't like the fact that more and more Christians were popping up everywhere around him. So, he secluded himself from the growing Christian community, myself included. He tried to pretend that we didn't exist – keeping an aura of traditionalism that he thought would keep the people contented."

**The Conversion of King Mirian**

"One day while he was out hunting, and his thoughts were wandering, he resolved to purge the kingdom of the vile Christian influence. He decided that all those who followed the Christian religion, and would not renounce it when ordered to do so, should be killed. Even his wife, Queen Nana, would face the death penalty if she failed to renounce the Christian Faith. This was pretty extreme, but the king was determined and intransigent."

"But when deep in the woods, he suddenly realized that he had become separated from the rest of the hunting party, and was lost. What's more, it was getting darker and darker, wild animals seemed to be surrounding him, and an awesome hail and rain storm with horrific thunder and lightning, was commencing (similar to the one that had destroyed his pagan idols after I had prayed fervently to God, a few years earlier). He called out to his fellow hunters, but nobody could hear him. The darkness became so great that he couldn't see anything – not even the hand in front of his face – it was like he was blind. He became disoriented, lost his balance, and fell to the ground. The world seemed to be closing in on him, and he feared for his life. Thoughts of persecuting Christians were replaced by thoughts of self-preservation.

"He called out to the pagan gods of his ancient religion, but there was no answer – they had deserted him.

"Then, in a desperate state, he thought back to his wife's miraculous healing, and her conversion to the new religion, the god of Nino: *If indeed this person named Jesus Christ, whom the captive girl had preached to my wife, was really the one God, then let Him now deliver me from this dreadful darkness, that I too might forsake all other gods and worship Him.*

"And with that thought, he prayed out loud with utter conviction:

> *I pray to the god of Nino, the runaway slave, who has attended to my wife and comforted her. Here and now, I am lost and in despair – I am in trouble and fear for my life! The gods of my ancestors have not answered my call, and I am afraid that I may die alone in these woods. If indeed, the god of Nino, this Jesus Christ, is the one true God, then I ask Him now to deliver me from this frightful darkness – illumine the night for me and guide my footsteps home. If He will do this, then I will be forever grateful, and I will forsake all other gods. I will declare His holy Name, and the related Good News, and spread it throughout the kingdom. I will erect a cross and venerate it, and I will construct a temple in honor of Him. I vow to be obedient to Nino's teaching and to the Faith of the Roman people.*[14] *In Jesus' Name – in Jesus' Name – hear me now! Amen! Amen!*[15]

"As soon as he finished his prayer, the light of day began to shine again, and he could see once more; the night was transfigured and the sun shone radiantly. His disorientation was gone, and he knew his way back home. Right then, King Mirian gave great thanks to whom he called the 'God of Nino', and vowed to accept the Christian faith. Renewed and invigorated, he hastily returned to his palace."

"Almost immediately after arriving back at his home, he requested an audience with me, and I reported at once.

'You are the runaway slave girl that I've heard so much about. You have healed many people of their afflictions – and you have healed my wife of a dreadful illness. For this, I give you my sincere gratitude. Your name is Nino, yes?'

'Yes, your highness. I am at your service.'

'Through God's mighty power you're skilled in healing,

like the daughter of Armazi.'

'Your highness, I know nothing about your gods or their daughters.' I wanted to say "false gods", but I held my tongue in check, not knowing what he wanted.

'I am only a mortal woman, and a humble servant of the God I put my belief in – the one true and almighty God in heaven.'

'But who is this Jesus Christ? Is he another god?'

'Not at all,' I said to him. 'There is only one true God, but He exists as three Persons simultaneously – God the Father, God the Son, and God the Holy Spirit. All three are 100% God, but there is only one God. Jesus Christ, our Lord, is God the Son, the Only-begotten Son of the Father. Belief in Him is our gateway to heaven and eternal life.'

"He seemed interested, so I continued to explain the Christian faith in more detail, and the Christian worship practices we follow. Then, he told me about his life-changing experience in the woods – and he became very solemn and respectful. He told me everything – the whole story of becoming lost, getting caught in the storm, and praying to God – 'my God' – for help. And his sudden rescue and enlightening. He vowed to change his life, and embrace the new faith. Not only that, but he wanted his entire household to become Christians – which included his son Rev II, his son Aspacures II,[16] and a daughter whose name I can't remember. And I believed him.

"The next day, King Mirian and his two sons and daughter, converted to Christianity.[17] I baptized them all in the Name of the Father, and of the Son, and of the Holy Spirit. Queen Nana watched and was tearful with joy. It was a wondrous occasion."[18]

## NOTES

---

1. the Javakheti Mountains

2. Lake Paravani

3. Armazi was the supreme divinity – the chief of the gods – and the central figure in the official pagan religion of Caucasian Iberia (eastern Georgia). The origin of this deity may be loosely connected with the Zoroastrian supreme being, Ahura-Mazda. Zaden was the god of fertility in the official pagan pantheon, and he was believed to be just as powerful as Armazi. His statue was said to have been destroyed, along with the statues of Armazi and other lesser gods, through the prayers of Saint Nino.

4. Urbnisi is now a village in Georgia's Shida Kartli region, in the district of Kareli. Situated on a high left bank of the Mtkvari river, it was an important city in ancient and early medieval Iberia (as today's Republic of Georgia was known to the Greeks and Romans). It was the second most important city in the Iberian Kingdom after the capital Mtskheta. After the nation's conversion to Christianity, it became a major center of Orthodox culture, and a seat of the bishop.

5. Rumor has it that King David the Builder (1089-1125) was a descendant of the boy saved by Saint Nino, but this is just speculation.

6. Today, the Jvari (Cross) Monastery, exists on the site, so named because it contains the cross raised up by Saint Nino herself.

7. Note the irony here: Nino was also emotionally attached – although in a negative way – to the thorny rose bush, because of her experience in the garden outside the community's winery shelter, where all of her friends and fellow Christians met their untimely deaths at the hands of King Tiridates.

8. Some records indicate the affliction may have been leukemia.

9. This was not a full body immersion, which was the common practice at the time. Protocols mandated an altered approach where only the head was immersed. Nino's baptisms were a harbinger of today's 'more modest' baptismal practices.

10. Nino's prayer is an early version of the Apostle's Creed.

11. Nana was Mirian's second wife.

12. Mirian III established peaceful relations with the Roman emperor Constantine the Great and the Armenian King Tiridates III, after Constantine declared Christianity as an acceptable religion of the empire. As a result of

---

Mirian's established relations, he arranged for Rev II to marry Salome in ~326 AD for political goodwill. Through marriage, Salome became a Queen of Iberia, and co-ruled with Rev II and her in-laws from 345 until 361 AD.

13. Salome and Perozhavra were genuinely able to assist Saint Nino in spreading the Christian faith since they were women of influential social status, being the wives of nobility.

14. as opposed to the faith of the Persian people, the other celebrated religious tradition that had swept the land many years ago

15. King Mirian made one of those well-known deals with God, offering to convert and be repentant if he survived. Such 'deals' are the inverse of the pious way of conversing with God. But they are nevertheless heard by God, and answered within the big picture of divine universal love. The king basically said, "If you do something for me now, then I'll do something for you later," a typical non-pious self-centered approach. The inverse of that would be, "If I do something for you now (believe in the Lord Jesus Christ as your personal Savior), then I hope that you'll do something for me later (give you everlasting life)". Of course, a more humble and pious approach would be for one to say something like, "My God, I praise You, and thank You for Your gift of creation, and I believe that my Lord Jesus Christ sacrificed His earthly life on the cross to atone for my sins, such that I may hopefully one day share eternal life with You in heaven."

16. also known as Varaz-Bakur (or Bakar)

17. Historical accounts put the year of King Mirian's conversion to Christianity at ~334 AD. Mirian declared Christianity as Iberia's state religion in ~337 AD. The dates differ slightly in various accounts.

18. For many years, the royal household continued to zealously aid Nino in all her missionary efforts.

# 6 IBERIA – THE LATER YEARS

*By the rolling of dice, the Robe of Christ was allotted to a Roman soldier, sold to a Christian convert, and then brought to Iberia as a present – but it was buried and lost.*

**THE SETTING:** On her deathbed, Nino is relating her life story to her friends Salome and Perozhavra.

**THE STORY LINE:** Nino lives in a hut in a garden on the grounds of the royal palace of the king of Iberia. She has preached the Gospel to many – healing the sick, comforting the downhearted, and converting the heathen. Through her prayers and intercession with God, she has saved a dying infant, aided a couple to conceive a child, healed the queen from a terminal illness and brought her to Christ, helped save the king from a horrible death, and then converted him and the royal family to Jesus Christ, our Lord. But her mission is not yet completed.

## THE ROBE OF CHRIST

"**IT** was my guardian Sara, who first told me about the Robe of Christ. How by the rolling of dice, it was allotted to a Roman soldier, then sold to a Christian convert, and finally brought to Iberia as a present for a sibling. But it was subsequently buried and lost. I was fascinated by the story, and dreamed of being able to come here someday and search for the Robe myself – and hopefully, to find it, by the grace of God! As you know, I never forgot that story, or lost that desire."

"One day, during my general sermonizing, I got talking to some Jewish people who claimed to know where the Robe was located. That perked up my ears, and I diligently tried to pry out the details. They said that they were the descendants of a man called Elias, who had changed his name to Elioz when he became a Christian.

"Elioz was a trader by vocation, and he was the person who had bought the Robe from the Roman soldier who had won it at the foot of the cross. Since it was a one-piece tunic,[1] he thought that it might have some value, such that he could sell it at a profit. But when he touched it and held it close to his heart, he felt an overwhelming sense of peace and contentment. So, instead of selling it, he decided to give it to his sister, who was suffering badly from some form of anxiety disorder. When he next traveled home to Iberia, he brought the Robe with him and gave it to his suffering sister, who was named Sidonia, as a gift. But before he returned, because of the effect of the Robe on his own character and disposition, he converted and became a Christian.

"When he presented the Robe to Sidonia, and she clasped it to her chest, she fell into a swoon of ecstasy. It was like nothing he had ever seen before. She was enraptured with overwhelming emotions caused by coming into contact with something so sacred. But alas, it was to be her last hurrah. Her condition had worsened in his absence, and unfortunately, she could no longer regulate her senses, respiration, and metabolism in such a rapt state. Intimate contact with the sacred Robe of Christ was too much for her disposition,[2] and her heart started racing beyond control.

Tightly clutching the Robe, Sidonia sadly died in a deep state of euphoria.

"When Elioz tried to take possession of the garment, he was overcome with fright and alarm when he could not withdraw it from her arms, so firmly did she hold the garment to her breast when she passed away. And no one else could take the robe from her either.

"It so happens that this event caused a great stir in Mtskheta, and even reached the ears of the King [3]– who was also unable to extract the Robe. Elioz properly realized that he should not tamper with a divinely guided state of affairs, and buried Sidonia with the Robe tightly pressed to her chest, with full Christian honors.

"Many years later, the great-nephew of the king who had touched the Robe,[4] looked for the tunic among the Jewish population of the city, but had failed to find it or learn much about it, except that it was buried near a cedar tree,[5] to the east of the city center and by a small bridge." [6]

"And that's all the descendants of Elioz could tell me. They didn't know the precise location of the tree. They thought that it might now be in the royal gardens, since they were east of the city center, and over the years, more and more land had been appropriated by the king for royal residences and the surrounding grounds.

"Of course, I became excited because I thought I knew where this bridge might be. So, I went to that area of the grounds, looked all around, and found a small bridge. And sure enough, a huge tree of cedar had grown just off the path and close to the bridge. I ran off to get Levan and a couple of shovels, and we returned to the site of the tree. Together, we dug in the ground by the roots of the tree, for about two hours. Admittedly, I had some doubts about whether this was the correct tree, but I was driven to find out. And then, just when we were about to give up, we hit something.

"It was a coffin. Realizing that we were acting on the edge of impropriety – although there was no marking or gravestone to be found – we decided to break open the coffin. And at that moment, a bright beam of light, from an otherwise cloud-filled overcast sky, shone on the bodily remains of a young girl, and on the undecomposed garment clutched in her hands to her chest. Levan and I looked at each other in amazement, and there was a moment of epiphany when we both sensed that a divine energy had been released. It was a defining moment in our lives, where we felt that we were one with God, and would never again be separated from Him.

"I had found the Robe of Christ!"

## THE LIVING PILLAR

"**WE** knew that this was a sacred and holy site, and should not be further disturbed or desecrated. So, we carefully covered the precious find, and rushed off to speak with the king.

"When we finally got his audience, and explained to him what we had found, he was almost giddy with joy and excitement. He wanted to build a memorial on the site immediately, but the queen insisted that it must be a full-fledged chapel. I suggested that we build a church – the country's first official church. And so, it was decided. The next day, King Mirian commissioned construction of the first Christian church, built over the grave of Sidonia, and containing the Robe of Christ." [7]

"Over the next few weeks, I worked with the royal engineers on the design of the church, because they were clueless on how a Christian church should be laid out.

Following what I remembered from Roman basilicas, we used a rectangular plan with entrance at one end and a dome-like semicircular apse at the other end. The main floorspace was divided into a wide nave – or central space – with lower roofed aisles along each side. The altar was centrally placed at the junction of nave and apse. Between the altar and the congregational area was a space for use by a choir. We placed two ambos – or pulpits – at the sides of the choir space for the reading of Scripture. The church was approached through a porch – or narthex – which was like an enclosed atrium. Penitents and those without church membership could listen to the services from the narthex." [8]

"A few months later, work started on the structure of the new church. The giant cedar tree by the gravesite was cut down and sawed into logs, for use as the main structural vertical beams or columns (or pillars). Seven structural columns were made from the cedar tree.

"Slowly, and with great effort, six of the columns were erected into their prescribed positions on the ground plan.

"But for some unknown reason, the seventh column could not be put in place. It just wouldn't go where it was supposed to go. The workers tried everything they could, but it just couldn't be positioned into its rightful place. After each attempt, it was left suspended horizontally by ropes above the installation site. It was as if it 'floated' above the site.

"When I was told of the problem, I prayed all night for the column to be set properly in place, such that the building of the church could continue in earnest – and when completed, all people would be able to seek comfort and hope with our Lord Jesus Christ, in fellowship in a holy church dedicated to Him.

"The next day, the workers tried again to set this last column in its designated spot. Suspended horizontally by ropes, the mighty column perilously swayed back and forth in the air. In the misty haze of the morning, the ropes were almost invisible, and it appeared as if it was a living tree branch wavering to-and-fro in the wind. The workers were very concerned and wanted to abort the operation. But then suddenly, and quite marvelously, the column somehow just smoothly rotated, glided to the correct spot, and was rightly slipped into its proper place.

"A crowd of people were watching, and it appeared to them to just miraculously transform from a horizontal pillar swinging in space to a vertical column firmly set in its base. The crowd was amazed and cheered loudly. The workers beamed with pride. As for me, it felt really good to see the last foundational structure properly set in place. Now, the walls, roof, and interior work could begin with conviction – and soon we would have a holy place for worship." [9]

"Within days, word had spread all around the city of how the 'living pillar' was brought into place by my prayers to Jesus Christ. Maybe so – I was just thankful and relieved. I only know that God was with us that day, and for that I am forever grateful. And the people have been brought one step closer to Christ. Amen."

## THE ENLIGHTENING OF A NATION

"**AFTER** the basic structure of the church was complete, the people were clamoring for more instruction in the faith – more knowledge of the history, more understanding of the practices, and more insight into salvation and everlasting life. In other words, they zealously yearned to experience the fullness of the faith. I couldn't do it all – joyfully, it had become a popular movement. So, I advised King Mirian to send an ambassador – on behalf of the entire nation – to emperor Constantine in Byzantium with a petition, informing him of our conversion and our church, and requesting that bishops and priests be sent to Iberia to complete the work that God had begun." [10]

"After all the exhilarating work of spreading the Gospel, converting the people, setting up the church, and comforting the faithful, I was exhausted, and realized that I could no longer work the royal gardens and work my precious ministry with equal fervor. My passion was with the ministry, so at length, reluctantly, I bade farewell to Levan, the king and queen, and to all my friends – especially the two of you – and withdrew to a more private residence in the mountains – where I could meditate and pray in solitude – thanking God for everything that He had done in the world, and for everything that He had done for me. I'm so happy that you came often to visit me – where we could plan what to do next, and reflect on all the good work that was being done on converting the pagans to our Lord. I'm so thankful that you two kept up the noble work of spreading the Good News throughout the kingdom."

**The Last Journey**

"I remember that a few years later you came to me, and together we went to the region of Kakheti in the east, where the pagans were still in the majority. We met a lot of resistance, but we also met a lot of people willing to listen to the Way, the Truth, and the Life.[11] Your help was instrumental in spreading the Light, and in teaching the queen all about our Lord and Savior. I remember the many sessions we had in the town square, in the friendly homes and workplaces, and in the royal courtyard. I remember the healings, the casting out of demons, and the comforting of the downhearted and dejected. And of course, I remember telling the story of the 'living pillar' over and over again to throngs of curious people.

"I thank God that Jacob 'the Priest' was with us, and helped with the sermons and the baptizing. I don't think we could have done it without him – God bless his soul. And I will never forget when Queen Sofia made her vow of faith,[12] and hinted that the royal court should do the same. That was a marvelous and incredible day.

"Remember when we went down into the valley just outside the main town, where there was a beautiful clear stream of running water? Thousands followed us, and Jacob baptized them all, including Queen Sofia, and her entire royal entourage. It was truly a stream of healing water [13]– thousands were healed, physically, spiritually, and emotionally. What an amazing sight! Witnessing so many people singing, praying, and praising God with all of their hearts, souls, and minds, in the beautiful lush valley by the stream of sparkling fresh clean water – it stirred my heart."

"And then, I remember confessing to you that I was tired, and my strength was ebbing. I needed to rest in a quiet place where I could meditate, pray, and give thanks to God. There was a hut on the mountainside near the village of Bodbe that fit the bill. So, we went there together, and there I took my leave of you both."

## NOTES

---

1. John 19:23-24

2. It is believed that Sidonia suffered from epilepsy.

3. King Aderc, according to some sources

4. a man named Armazael, according to some sources

5. a tree of Lebanon cedar

6. Later, this small bridge was called 'the bridge of the Magi'.

7. The church was not completed until 379 AD.

8. Early Christian church buildings were adapted from the existing common form of the Roman basilica (the so-called 'basilican church'). It admirably fulfilled its function as a building for the celebration of the Eucharist and the Holy Word.

9. The Svetitskhoveli Cathedral (which means 'living pillar') in Mtskheta, currently stands on the site of the first church building. The Cathedral is overlooked by Jvari (cross) Monastery, situated on a cliff above the town. The Monastery is so named because it contains the wooden cross raised up on the site by Saint Nino herself.

10. Records indicate that Constantine was elated, and a delegation of bishops was sent to the court of the Iberian King amid rejoicing and ceremony.

11. John 14:6

12. Queen Sofia was sometimes called 'Soggy'.

13. Today, In the valley to the northeast of the Bodbe Monastery, runs the magical river of healing water that has been affectionately dubbed the 'Source of St Nino'. A baptistery and a small church were built there in the name of her parents, Saints Zabulon and Susanna. A never-ending stream of pilgrims visit the site.

# EPILOGUE

*You are our beloved teacher, healer, and comforter – you have freed our souls – and for this we will never forget you.*

Nino is concluding the telling of the story of her life to her friends Salome and Perozhavra:

"**AND** that, my dear friends, is the story of my life. I've told it exactly as I remember it – no frills or exaggerations. You know that I desire neither honor or fame – it is enough to be content, knowing that I have used the gifts given to me by God, to the best of my ability, to praise the glory of Jesus Christ, our Lord and Savior. God has been good to me, and I thank Him ever so graciously for giving me this opportunity to do His work on earth – to bring people to the true faith – and to further the glory of His eternal Kingdom.

"I am tired now and need to sleep. We will be together again soon."

Kneeling by her bedside and weeping bitterly, Salome and Perozhavra leaned close and whispered, "We have listened carefully to everything you have said – we will remember it all, and it will be written down for everyone to know and learn from. We will tell all the holy believers about your life in the service of God – and we will continue to preach the Gospel of Jesus Christ to all the people in the land. You are our beloved teacher, healer, and comforter – you have freed our souls – and for this we will never forget you."

With that, Nino closed her eyes and drifted off into eternal sleep. She died a few hours later, contented and at peace.

Praise be to God.

## LEGACY

IN accordance with her will, Nino was buried, in the place where she took her last breath – in the mountainside village of Bodbi. King Mirian later erected a church in honor of Saint George over her grave. In the 9$^{th}$ century, the church was enlarged to a 3-nave basilica, and became the Bodbi Monastery. Her tomb is still shown in this Monastery. Today, the convent of the "Holy 'Equal-to-the-Apostles' Nino" operates on the site.

Her grapevine cross was sent to the cathedral in Mtskheta. During the wars between the Byzantine and Persian empires, the cross was taken to Armenia and eventually to Moscow. Czar Alexander I returned it to Georgia at the beginning of the 19th century.

Saint Nino has become one of the most venerated saints of the Georgian Orthodox Church, and her characteristic article, the grapevine cross, is a symbol of Georgian Christianity. Icons of Saint Nino are usually shown with her holding her grapevine cross, the pledge of her relationship with the Virgin Mary.

Saint Nino is called 'Equal-to-the-Apostles' because she preached the gospel in Georgia with equal passion and conviction as the first century Apostles Andrew,

Bartholomew, and Simon. Since the 17th century, many icons have been made showing her with the scroll she received in her second miraculous vision. Her title, her cross, and her scroll are the manifestations of her service to God in spreading the Gospel to all of the people in a strange new land.

The Orthodox Church commemorates Saint Nino's Day twice a year – late May/early June as the day she arrived in Georgia,[1] – and late January as the day she died.[2]

She is celebrated in the Roman Martyrology on December 15 under the name Saint Christiana.

*Thus did a powerless slave woman – strong in faith, will, and determination, but oppressed by the harsh twists-and-turns of life – by the power of Almighty God – convert an entire nation to the one true God and the one true Faith.*

Alleluia!

Thanks be to God!

**NOTES**

---

1. May 19 – June 1, per different calendars at different times

2. January 14 – January 27, per different calendars at different times

# APPENDIX I – MAPS

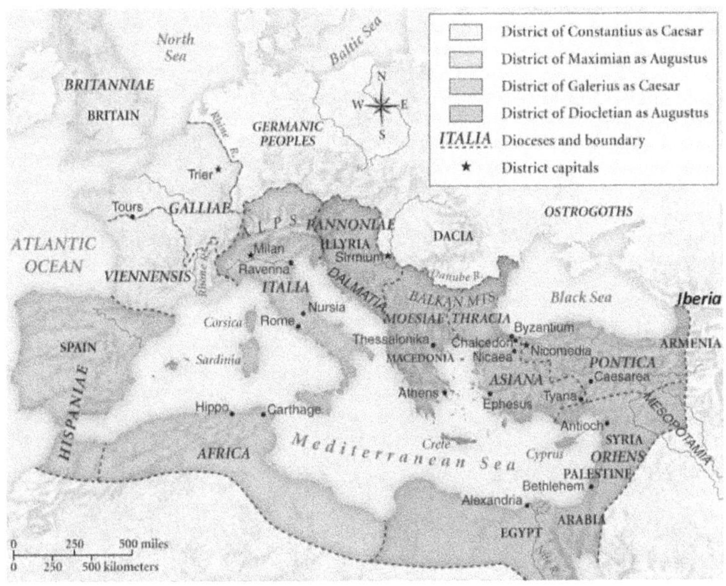


Roman Empire during the first Tetrarchy

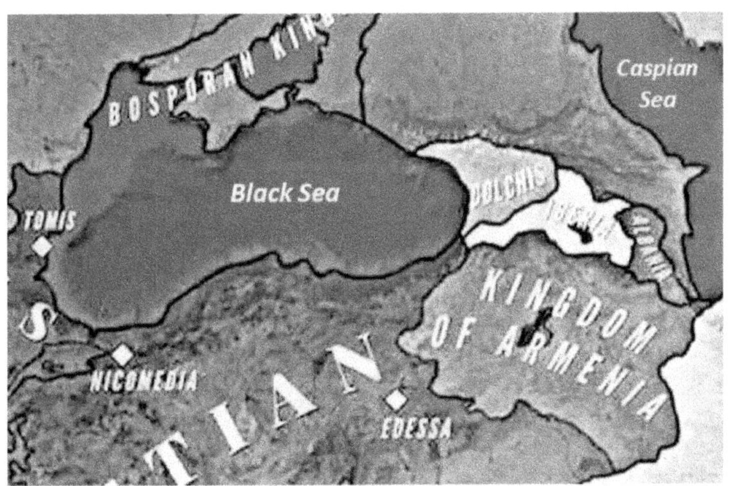


Kingdoms of Armenia, Iberia, Colchis, and Albania

APPENDIX II

# The Legacy of Saint Hripsime

**AFTER** the release of Gregory from prison and the conversion of King Tiridates to Christianity, chapels were built over the relics of the martyred ascetic community. In later years, during the time of Saint Sahag Bartev, these chapels were rebuilt, and during the pontificate of Bishop Gomidas (c. 618 AD), two beautiful churches were erected and the grounds consecrated. One of these, the Church of Saint Hripsime in Echmiadzin (Vagharshapat), continues to this day as a monument of Armenian faith, history, and architecture. Saint Hripsime, along with her companions in service to Christ, are venerated as holy martyrs in Armenian history.

In 1979, His Holiness Vasken I, the 'Catholicos (Bishop) of All Armenians', reported that as a result of recent archaeological excavations at the Church of Saint Hripsime, firmly sealed graves were found and thought to be those of the saints, Hripsime and her holy companions.

According to legend, Christ designated the spot for the shrine by descending from heaven in a shaft of light and striking the ground with a golden hammer until the earth shook.

Some of the saint's relics, along with items relating to King Tiridates and Gregory the Illuminator, were pillaged by Persians during an invasion in 1604, but were restored in 1638.

Other Christian traditions also commemorate Saint

Hripsime and her companion virgin martyrs: The Coptic Orthodox call her 'Saint Arapsima'. The Greek Orthodox venerate her as 'Saint Ripsimia'. The Ethiopian Orthodox call her 'Saint Arsema' - where she is very popular, with at least three church buildings named after her.

In honor of the saint, Hripsime remains a fairly common female name in Armenia, as do its variants; likewise, Arsema is a very popular name among Ethiopian Christians.

The Armenian Orthodox Church remembers Hripsime in early June (traditionally June 4). Gayane and her companions are commemorated separately soon after (traditionally on June 5). All 35 of the community of virgins were canonized, including Nino (as Saint Nune).

In the Roman Catholic tradition, Hripsime and her companions are commemorated with a feast day in late September (traditionally September 29). The Greek Orthodox, and the Orthodox Church in America, commemorate them usually the following day (traditionally September 30).

## About the Author:

Edward N Brown is a storyteller with a background in science, philosophy, history, and theology. His technique is to blend the interesting nuggets of myth, science, biography, history, design, romance, poetry, spirituality, and personal drama – all mixed together into an informative, but easy-reading, faith-based tale of inspiration and wonder. Years of personal study exploring the great mysteries that connect the secular with the spiritual, coupled with an educational background of three advanced degrees (PhD + two MS) with a focus on systems theory, have contributed to his insights on History, Truth, Christianity, and the Human Condition. Classified as 'Inspirational Stories Embracing Christian Biblical History', his works represent a speculative fusion of style – one that will entertain, inform, and inspire readers of all ages.

Crystal Sea Press website: https://www.crystalseapress.com
Crystal Sea Press email: rystalse@crystalseapress.com
Amazon Author Page:
https://www.amazon.com/author/crystalseapress_enbrown
Goodreads Profile Page:
https://www.goodreads.com/author/show/19232863.Edward_N_Brown
Facebook Publisher Page:
https://www.facebook.com/Crystal-Sea-Press-106797100691990/
Twitter Handle: @edwardnbrown55

## Other Books by Edward N Brown:

*Passion of the Slave Girls*
*Saint, Martyr, Virgin, Slave: Faith and Freedom Forever*
*The Passion of Thecla: Faith and Fortitude*
*The Passion of Eve: Remembering the End*
*The Passion of Eve: Remembering the Beginning*
Revised Edition 2020
Original Edition 2019

(all books available in Paperback and e-book formats)

"I AM the ALPHA and the OMEGA," says the Lord God,
"the One who is and who was and who is to come,
the Almighty!"
"I AM the ALPHA and the OMEGA, the First and the Last,
the Beginning and the End!
Blessed are they who wash their robes so as to have free
access to the Tree of Life ..."

Revelation 1:8 and 22:13-14

CRYSTAL SEA PRESS

Inspirational Stories Embracing Christian Biblical History

www.ingramcontent.com/pod-product-compliance
Lightning Source LLC
LaVergne TN
LVHW020644100826
845148LV00012B/2335

* 9 7 8 1 7 3 6 7 7 1 2 4 2 *